Someone to turn to

 Publications

SOMEONE TO TURN TO:

the social worker's role and the role of front line staff
in relation to people with mental handicaps

Dorothy Atkinson

First published 1989

© **1989 BIMH Publications**

(BIMH Publications is the publishing office of the
British Institute of Mental Handicap, Registered Charity No. 264786)

Published and distributed by: **BIMH Publications,**
Foley Industrial Park,
Stourport Road,
Kidderminster,
Worcs. DY11 7QG

ISBN 0 906054 66 4

Typeset by: Action Typesetting Limited, Imperial House, Russell Street,
Gloucester GL1 1NE

Printed by: Birmingham Printers (1982) Ltd., Stratford Street North,
Birmingham B11 1BY

Contents

Preface

This book is an account of roles and relationships at the "front line" of services for people with mental handicaps. It is in two parts. The first part is based on the findings of a follow-up study of people discharged from mental handicap hospitals to independent living situations in the community. The research project revealed that social workers were key people in the lives of former hospital residents. Social workers saw themselves, and they were seen by people with mental handicaps, as authority figures, friendly officials, and sometimes as threats; but most often as "friends". The relationships were long-term and intense, they were personal and practical, and they were usually very informal.

The second part of the book looks at the implications of this study, not only for the social workers involved but for other people at the front line of services. The account which follows is about the roles, both formal and informal, that staff adopt in the lives of people with mental handicaps as service users and the relationships that develop between them.

Acknowledgements

My sincere thanks go first to the service users in this study, for the time they spent with me and the views and opinions which they freely shared. I am indebted to them.

In this context, I thank also my previous social work colleagues. They gave generously of their time and shared their experiences, observations, and insights with warmth and humour. Their first-hand detailed knowledge of the lives of the people with whom they worked was invaluable in this study, and I am most grateful for their help.

Thanks are due, too, to my many earlier colleagues, both in Taunton and Frome who, on behalf of Somerset Social Services Department, gave me generous help and encouragement in the execution of this research. I am grateful to the Department for its cooperation throughout this study and also to Somerset Health Authority for its cooperation with the project.

I am indebted to Jane Gibbons, then at the University of Southampton, for her personal help and encouragement. Finally, thanks to Christine Love for typing the manuscript with her usual skill and speed; and to Jan Walmsley and Ann Brechin for reading it and offering helpful comments.

DA

Part One

Research findings, roles, and relationships

CHAPTER ONE

Introduction: the front line of services

The scope of the book

Moving home is one of life's major changes. When "home" means hospital and "new home" means a flat or house in a local neighbourhood, then this major change takes on new dimensions. It is a time of transition, when the old and unfamiliar gives way to the new and untested. This is when people most need "someone to turn to"; for help, advice, and support.

For people with mental handicaps the story does not end with the move from hospital to house. That is only the beginning. The need for support continues as they begin to settle, put down roots, and take their place in their local community. The quality of people's everyday lives is largely determined by the range and type of their relationships. "Informal" contacts (like family, friends, colleagues, and neighbours) are needed just as much as "formal" support staff.

In the growing literature on community living some key informal contacts have been identified. These include: family (Atkinson and Ward, 1986, 1987; Malin, 1983); friends (Shearer, 1986; Atkinson and Ward, 1987; Atkinson, 1987); companions such as a home-based friend, partner, spouse, or other close tie (Atkinson and Ward, 1987; Atkinson, 1988); neighbours, shopkeepers, and acquaintances (Atkinson, 1986; de Kock et al., 1988; Felce, D., 1988). These "support networks" may be crucial in determining how people adapt to living in the community and, in particular, the quality of their lives (Edgerton and Bercovici, 1976; Atkinson, 1986).

Other people matter too. They include the staff members who visit, or live in, the houses, flats, and group homes which are increasingly becoming part of local residential services. Formal support staff play a large part in the day-to-day lives of people with mental handicaps. They often hold the key to enhancing or, in some cases, diminishing the quality of people's lives. They are at the front line of services (Towell, 1985).

This book is set at the front line of services. The research on which it is based focused on social workers and their relationships with service users: in this case, people with mental handicaps living independently in the community. The issues which arise from the study, however, are not specific either to this branch of social work or even to social work itself. Other front line staff, such as community nurses, home helps, and other support workers, are likely to identify with the dilemmas, doubts, and conflicts which are highlighted in this account.

Thus the formal support workers at the front line in this account are social workers. The support they offer is practical, financial, and emotional. Their work with people with mental handicaps discharged into the community has similarities with the social worker's role in other areas and it has direct links with the casework or counselling skills used in supportive work with other client groups. The tasks carried out by the social workers in this study are ones which will also be recognised by other front line staff engaged in supporting people with mental handicaps living "independently" in the community.

Life at the front line: an overview

The frequency and closeness of contact between front line staff and service users ensures that relationships develop between them. These relationships can have an impact on people's lives, so great that front line staff can be seen as: "a valuable resource" (Porterfield, 1985), "the main resource" (Towell, 1985), "the most important resource" (Mansell and Porterfield, 1986), or even "the most valuable resource" (Porterfield, 1987).

Who are these people? And what do they do? There is a growing body of literature about:

the *selection* of staff, including people with "enthusiasm, determination and commitment" (Shearer, 1986) and those with local links and personal networks (Thomas, 1985; Firth, 1986);

the *induction, training, and support* of staff (Tyne, 1981; Mathieson, *et al.,* 1983; Porterfield, 1983, 1985; Ward, 1985; Mansell and Porterfield, 1986; Porterfield, 1987);

the *day-to-day tasks* of staff and their involvement in the lives of service users (Malin, 1983; Faire, 1985; Evans, *et al.,* 1985;

Shearer, 1986; Flynn, 1987; Humphreys, Evans, and Todd, 1987).

When a project is described or reported in the literature it is relatively easy to specify: the number of staff involved; their title, status, and formal role; and the frequency of their contact with service users. It is much more difficult to capture details of the *relationships* between staff and service users. This book sets out to do just that.

Who are the people in the front line?

There are many people in the front line of human services. Local mental handicap services are developing to meet local needs, and different health authorities, social services departments, housing associations, and voluntary organisations are appointing staff with various names and titles. Some staff visit people's homes and provide a domiciliary service. Others sleep or live in the homes of people with mental handicaps and provide a residential service.

Front line workers include:

social workers (and social work assistants);

community nurses;

home helps;

care assistants;

support workers;

key workers;

occupational therapists (and occupational therapy aides and assistants);

community service volunteers (CSVs);

home support officers;

home makers;

residential care workers; and,

nurses (and nursing assistants).

People who work in small, dispersed houses in the community have much in common with one another, regardless of role, title, or background. They have direct involvement in people's everyday home lives; and opportunities to develop close relationships with them. The issues they face within these relationships may well be the same as those highlighted for social workers in this account of domiciliary work. No doubt this book will be of interest to residential staff too as the dilemmas, doubts, and concerns do cut across the boundary between domiciliary and residential occupations. But it is primarily an account of the relationships that develop between people with mental handicaps living in their own homes and the staff who visit them.

What do front line staff do?

Staff titles, and their prescribed roles, do vary. There is, however, considerable overlap. The formal role of staff may include the teaching, or doing, of a range of specific tasks and activities.

Most residential staff and many domiciliary staff, such as home helps and care assistants, are involved in day-to-day household tasks. They may demonstrate or teach various essential domestic tasks, such as cooking, washing, ironing, and cleaning; or they may participate actively in these activities, working alongside people who need help with them. There are both teaching and doing elements in this role.

Front line staff, therefore, help to teach people who can benefit from learning new skills. They also provide support to people who cannot acquire such new skills by being around to do these everyday tasks with them or on their behalf.

The same teaching or doing principle applies to a range of personal, social, domestic, and community activities. Thus front line staff may be called on to give help with:

self-care skills;

laundry, cleaning, shopping, and cooking;

personal finances;

personal relationships (getting on with others and making friends);

day time and leisure activities (participation in the neighbourhood and making contact with local people).

Life at the front line: the social context

The performance of a range of set tasks and activities is not as straightforward as it might at first seem. Staff are not simply working through daily checklists, where each task is ticked off on completion and they move on to the next one. In practice they are "working in new, untested ways, living intimately and intensively with maybe very handicapped or disturbed individuals, isolated from traditional means of support" (Ward, 1983). The "help" they provide may not be appreciated by people who experience it as "interference". It may, in practice, be no easier for a front line worker to relinquish control and take risks, than it is for a parent in the family home or a nurse in a hospital.

The job of offering support, in whatever practical or emotional ways, is fraught with difficulty. It does not take place in a social vacuum. It has to be done in the context of people's homes, where it impinges on their lives, life styles, and views about themselves. It runs the risk of real, or imagined, misunderstandings because feelings and emotions are aroused on both sides.

This book is about that social context. It looks at the roles people adopt and the relationships that develop between them. The details of day-to-day interactions between staff and service users, and the nature of their regular encounters, is often missing from the literature. This book attempts to contribute to this area of knowledge. The discussion goes beyond a description of formal roles and moves into the realm of relationships between people, their perceptions and feelings about one another, and the informal roles that members of staff, over time, may come to adopt.

The social context is important on both sides. Issues for service users arising from the research, which will be considered later, include dependency, exclusivity, and friendship. These issues are important for staff too, as are their personal responses towards service users and any feelings they may have of isolation, vulnerability, or responsibility. Staff training and support is needed, not only to counteract these feelings but, more positively, to develop in staff an enabling and facilitative role. A key task for well-trained and supported staff is in helping service users create and develop close and positive relationships with others.

A detailed account follows which illustrates these points. It is based on the findings of a two-part research project which first identified its research population from hospital records and then followed people up in their community settings. The remainder of Part One of this book is a presentation of some of the findings from the follow-up study. It looks at the roles adopted by social workers and at the relationships they developed, over time, with the people with mental handicaps with whom they worked – the service users.

Part Two of the book then broadens the discussion to include other staff groups. It looks critically at the findings of the research study and draws out the implications; not only for social workers but also for others at the front line of services.

CHAPTER TWO

The research project

Aims of the study

In a classic study in the field of mental handicap, Edgerton (1967) states that: "the ex-patient succeeds in his efforts to sustain a life in the community only as well as he succeeds in locating and holding a benefactor". More recently, in a study in this country, Malin (1983) suggests that the social worker is an important source of help to people living in the community. He found, in his study of six group homes in Sheffield, that the residents depended mainly on the support provided through official networks. He looked at their contact with relatives, neighbours, friends, and official support workers; and found the latter group to be particularly important.

Who do people turn to when living in the community? Do they, as Edgerton suggests, recruit a benefactor? Or is the social worker the key support figure in their lives? Or are the two roles interchangeable? Do social workers take on the attributes of "benefactors"?

This study looks at the role of social workers working with people with mental handicaps in the community.

Background

The social worker's role in working with the families of children and adults with mental handicaps has received some attention over the years (for example: Hewett, 1970; Bayley, 1973; Hanvey, 1981; Browne, 1982). The role of the social worker in the lives of people with mental handicaps living independently, however, has received relatively little attention.

There is some interest now in direct work with people with mental handicaps in the community. For example, Anderson (1982) notes the social worker's possible involvement in the selection and preparation of people for independent living, and in facilitating their move from hospital to group home. In his study, Malin (1983) indicated that the social worker continues to have a role *after* the selection, preparation, and move of people from hospital to community.

What is that continuing role? The present author elsewhere uses a client's phrase "right hand person" to summarise the social worker's role in helping people with mental handicaps to live independently in the community: "The social worker as a right hand person needs to form a relationship which is based on regular and reliable contact, and which is long-term. Within this context, there will be practical help both in the home and in the wider community, and usually this will incorporate a teaching element, as well as the fun or challenge of doing things together"(Atkinson, 1982).

There is more to this role than doing, teaching, and having fun. There is likely to be, as Gilbert (1985) notes, a personal counselling role and the use of casework skills, albeit in imaginative and innovative ways.

The research

A rehabilitation scheme was set up in Somerset following the publication, in 1971, of the government White Paper, *Better Services for the Mentally Handicapped.* This saw a key role for social workers in helping people with mental handicaps live in the community. It stated that some people would be able to live "in ordinary housing or a group home or flatlets with social work support" (para 159). Similarly, it stated: "Given someone to turn to for help with problems of ordinary life many mentally handicapped people can achieve considerable independence . . ." (para 165). The social worker was thought to be that "someone".

The Somerset minimum support group programme built on the principles set out in the White Paper. The social worker was seen to be the key person in the rehabilitation scheme; the person who would provide support to people discharged from long-stay hospitals. This study looks at the nature and quality of that support, and considers whether the social worker is, in practice, "someone to turn to".

The respondents

Members of the research group were identified from hospital records. Every person discharged from the three Somerset mental handicap hospitals to an independent living situation during the decade 1971 – 1981, was automatically included. The group comprised fifty-five people, twenty-seven men and twenty-eight women, whose average age on leaving hospital was forty-eight years. Members' ages ranged from four people in their twenties at one end of the scale, to nine people aged sixty or more at the upper end of the scale. Their average length of stay in hospital was twenty-seven-and-a-half years; four having lived in hospital for five years or less, and eleven having lived in hospital for forty years or more.

In the period between discharge and follow-up one person had left the country and four people had died, leaving a group of fifty people available for follow-up. This final group of twenty-six men and twenty-four women were, at the time of the completion of fieldwork (May, 1983), aged between twenty-nine and seventy-four years. Some people had, by then, lived in their minimum support groups for nine or ten years; their average length of stay in independent living situations being six-and-a-half years.

Method

The fieldwork was carried out in the six-month period from November 1982 to May 1983. The information was collected from three sources: social services case notes; interviews with social workers; and interviews with service users.

Social services case notes

The detailed scrutiny of case notes allowed a retrospective look at social worker – service user contacts, sometimes over several years and, in some instances, involving previous social workers' accounts. Shared occasions, important events, and details of practical help were written up in the case notes. Actual letters and cards received from service users were often incorporated in the files. More recent, and current, events were also written about in case notes.

Interviews with social workers

Interviews with social workers were partly focused around the factual details of service users' current life styles. The interviews were also, in part, open ended; allowing social workers the opportunity to think about, and discuss, their own role. Social workers were invited to describe the kind of help and support they offered. They made their own personal assessment of their role, and described their social worker – service user relationship. All fourteen social workers participated in interviews with the researcher (present author) and the interviews were tape recorded.

Interviews with service users

Interviews with service users were also, in part, focused around the factual details of each person's current life style. They also offered opportunities for people to think about and discuss their social workers, past and present; how they saw them, what they did, and what they thought about them.

All fifty people in the research group were invited to participate in interviews, and forty-seven accepted the invitation. Social workers arranged the interviews, gave personal introductions where necessary and, in two instances, sat in on interviews to alleviate anxieties. Interviews, with one exception, were tape recorded.

Interview strategies were adopted which enabled people to talk freely about their lives. Open-ended questions were used, a friendly and informal atmosphere was established, and a conversational format was adopted. More details of the research methods used are given in Atkinson (1985) and (1988).

CHAPTER THREE

Living in the community

Discharge from hospital

The people in this study had lived in institutions for an average of twenty-seven-and-a-half years before being discharged into the community. A study of hospital case notes revealed their typical hospital "career". Typically this comprised compulsory admission, compulsory detention, institutionalisation, separation from home, and loss of contact with relatives.

In the period 1971 to 1981 a total of fifty-five people were discharged to independent living situations from three Somerset mental handicap hospitals. Forty-five of these people undertook a period of residential training, in a group setting, and moved into council houses in different parts of the county to form "minimum support groups". They were taught the skills deemed necessary for living independently in the community, including self-care, domestic, community, academic, and relationship skills.

The other ten people sidestepped the official rehabilitation scheme and went straight into homes of their choice. They did not undergo a comprehensive residential training programme and they did not go into minimum support groups. Instead they left hospital, at their own request, to set up their own homes with a partner, a friend, or alone.

Independent living situations

The term "independent living situation" is, in this study, an umbrella term. It includes minimum support groups, shared houses, marital homes, and single person dwellings.

The minimum support group, in 1971-1981, was Somerset Social Services Department's approved model for independent living. The model was linked with selection procedures and rehabilitation programmes, it carried a departmental budget, and it had a clearly established system of formal support. The model was described in detail in a separate section of the Department's handbook which set out: its aims; the departmental policy; the procedure for setting up groups; and detailed guidance on supporting the service users.

There was no equivalent handbook entry for the alternative option, chosen by the ten people who set up their own homes. Thus no policy statement, procedural outline, budget, or guidance was issued to social workers. This option was an alternative devised by service users themselves; people who opted for a more individualised and home-like setting, with a friend, marital partner, or alone. There were no linked training or rehabilitation programmes, no formal links with housing departments, and no established systems of formal support.

In order to provide a context for the later presentation of the research findings, the two patterns of living will now be described in some detail. The descriptions that follow are prototypes, or ideal types.

Minimum support groups

A minimum support group is "a mutually supportive group"* of adults with mental handicaps. In this study these tended to be four person groups, often comprising two men and two women. Selection of group members was undertaken by hospital and social services staff, who sought people whose skills and strengths were complementary and who were thought to be compatible as people. The aim was to foster a self-supporting small group. Each person had a contribution to make in actual skills and in social or interpersonal input. The four contributing parts made up a working whole; a viable unit of four people who, between them, could successfully run the household. Individually each member could draw on peer group support in order to run his or her own life.

Selection of candidates was based on the principles of peer group support and the interdependence of group members. The selected candidates were given a period of residential training in a specially designated unit. They were taught a variety of personal and domestic skills, and were encouraged to help and support one another, to share, and to cooperate amongst themselves.

---

*The information on which this account is based comes from: the entry on "Minimum Support Groups" in Somerset Social Services Department's departmental handbook; and a policy statement, "Minimum Support Groups for Mentally Handicapped People in Somerset", written in 1978.

At the end of the training period (which usually lasted between three and twelve months) the group would move to a council house in a town where members had some links or, at the very least, where they had no objection to living. Usually the house provided was a standard, three-bedroomed, family-type house on a housing estate, with access to shops and other amenities.

In the community the groups were expected to be self-supporting for most day-to-day personal and domestic matters. However, there was a complex formal support system to buttress them from major difficulties. The support offered was financial, domestic, and personal.

Financial support

Financial support to minimum support groups was of two types: major household grants; and day-to-day monitoring of individual incomes.

The first major household grant was made at the outset. This was a grant for the group members, with their social worker, to spend on furnishing and equipping the group home. In subsequent years funds were released to each group to enable them to replace items of furniture or equipment. Repairs of household items and materials for decorating could also be financed from the annual allocated sum.

The second form of financial support was the monitoring, or control, of essential weekly expenses. Somerset Social Services Department was the official tenant of the group home, and the group members were sub-tenants of the Department. The Department paid the rent, in advance, to the local district housing department, and then recouped the money by receiving weekly payments from group members. It was, therefore, difficult though not entirely unknown for group members to get into rent arrears. Similarly, lighting and heating charges were paid by the department, and an appropriate weekly fee was levied on individuals in order to recoup the money. Again it was virtually impossible for a group member to get into difficulties with electricity and gas charges. A telephone was provided to each group home. The telephone rental and official calls were covered by the departmental budget, but group members took some responsibility for paying for their own private calls.

The other major weekly expense was the shopping bill; the food, drink, and household items that were required by the group. The training programme prior to community living aimed to instil in group members the idea of the household kitty. Each person contributed an agreed amount each week, and the money was used to buy the essential shared commodities for the group and the household. The home help and/or the social worker ensured the continuance of the household kitty system and, where appropriate, gave advice on best buys and wise spending.

Any money remaining after meeting their share of the weekly expenses was for group members' own use. However, the value of saving money was inculated at the training stage, and the principles of saving were re-emphasised and reinforced in the community setting. People were encouraged to have personal savings accounts, and to save for clothes, outings, Christmas, and holidays. The aim was for each person to take responsibility for meeting his or her own needs, and to become self-sufficient.

Domestic support

A home help was allocated to each group. The departmental handbook states that the home help "will give guidance, support and encouragement with the day-to-day running of the household, not doing the cleaning for the group, but assisting with budgeting, planning the shopping, meals, etc.". In practice, home helps worked alongside group members helping and advising on many different household tasks, including shopping, washing, and ironing.

Personal support

Individual group members received personal support from two main sources. The home help offered informal advice on routine day-to-day matters while undertaking duties in the house. The main source of help and advice, however, was the group's social worker, whom group members could consult about any more personal difficulties. Such difficulties sometimes concerned an individual member's role, or status, within the group. In such instances the social worker would have to combine support with monitoring and control.

Social workers also contributed a practical input to minimum support groups. For example, they ensured that bills were paid, letters were answered, light bulbs were changed, the garden was kept tidy, and the house was kept clean and in good decorative order. They also kept a discreet eye on each group member's appearance, personal hygiene, general health, and personal wellbeing, offering advice as and when appropriate.

Own homes

The alternative to the minimum support group will be called "own homes". The first of these to be set up, by ten people, included a bungalow, a cottage, and one- and two-person flats. The households were small, typically comprising one or two people.

This alternative pattern of living had no stated aims or objectives. It reflected a preference, on the part of a few people, to leave hospital and set up home as independently as possible. There was no automatic progression through a residential training scheme and, therefore, some people had no training prior to discharge from hospital.

Applications were made by individuals to their local housing departments. The applicants became council tenants and had to pay rent, and conduct other business, directly and personally with the council. They were also consumers of gas and electricity, and had to deal directly with fuel boards. Tenants also dealt directly with other tradespeople and authorities, such as the milkman, the coalman, the local water board, and British Telecom.

There was no departmental budget for this option. People were expected to spend their own money, claim Social Security grants, and obtain furniture, furnishings, and equipment as cheaply as possible. They could be helped by cast-offs from family or neighbours, by donations from voluntary sources and charities, or they might inherit second-hand goods given to the social services area office. Replacement of items was by the same means, though sometimes social workers obtained small grants from central funds to assist them.

People choosing the own homes option retained responsibility for their personal finances. They had to learn, *in situ,* how to budget their fixed weekly income, pay their rent and bills, and try to save for extras. There was a great deal of leeway in this option and people could, and did, get into financial difficulty.

The support system was rudimentary. No telephone was provided, though people could choose to have one if they met the costs. There was no automatic entitlement to a home help. People did, however, have contact with a social worker, so some help and guidance was available on domestic, financial, and personal matters. There was "someone to turn to".

People choosing to set up their own homes were not taught any good housekeeping principles before leaving hospital and so they had not learned the rudiments of wise shopping, nor how to set aside money for essential expenses, including a food kitty, nor the practice of saving money for clothes, hobbies, and special occasions. From a regulated, routine, hospital environment where everything was provided for them, they moved into an unstructured, semi-autonomous, domestic setting where they had to create their own systems, their own routines, and their own ways of doing things.

The own homes option offered a large degree of autonomy and independence in an ordinary domestic setting. It was, however, thought to be a precarious way of life for people who had spent much time in institutions and who had little or no experience of community living. Thus, although there was an awareness that people would continue to need support, this type of living was not officially recognised as an option; and there was no automatic access to budgetary help, cash incentives, or domestic support.

Where were people at the time of the follow-up?

At the time of the completion of the follow-up field work, in May 1983, the fifty people remaining from the fifty-five who had been discharged were living as follows: twenty-six in minimum support groups; sixteen in their own homes; four in family settings; and four in institutional settings.

Everyone in the follow-up group had a current social worker. Many people had had previous ones too. In the study both social workers and people with mental handicaps talked about the social work role and described their relationships with each other. Their views, together with supplementary information from documentary sources, form the basis of the next four chapters.

CHAPTER FOUR

The social work task: an outline

Need for support

The people in the research group, in moving from long-term hospital care into the community, moved from an enclosed world and a protected environment into a relatively exposed and un-protected situation. As people with comparatively few skills, an assumed low level of academic achievement, and usually little actual experience of ordinary, small-scale domestic living, they faced what would seem to be a daunting prospect. Although they moved into "independent" living situations their continuing need for support was officially recognised, especially in the carefully planned minimum support groups. Even people choosing the own homes option were assumed to need, as a minimum provision, the continuing services of a social worker.

Each person left behind a familiar hospital routine, the predict-able days of institutional life, and a support network of peers, friends, and staff. It was certainly possible, and easily within each person's control, to re-establish at a domestic level a routinised and predictable home environment. But what of the personal support? Who, if anyone, replaced the support figures left behind in hospital?

From each individual's point of view, as an inexperienced and vulnerable person, support was very necessary. Modern living is complex, requiring a range of sophisticated technical, practical, and academic skills. There are appropriate and inappropriate ways of behaving, nuances in interactions, and a range of required inter-personal skills. Support figures were needed to provide both practical help and emotional and social support.

This chapter will begin to examine the social worker as a "support figure". It will look at the nature of the social work task and the elements which comprise it. Subsequent chapters will explore these elements in detail, and describe the relationships which developed between the people involved.

The social workers

The people in the research group appeared on the case loads of fourteen social workers, nine women and five men. Seven of these, or half of the group, were generic social workers; they formed the largest single group. The remaining seven comprised two social work assistants, four specialist social workers (two mental handicap specialists, one mental health specialist, and one blind specialist), and one team leader.

Social workers		Research group	
Number	Type	Number	Per cent
7	Generic	22	44
2	Social work assistants	8	16
2	Mental handicap specialists	13	26
3	Others	7	14
14		50	100

TABLE 1. Distribution of research group members between social workers.

As shown in Table 1, generic social workers formed the largest single group of social workers. They dealt with most research group members: twenty-two people, or 44 per cent of the total group. Generic social workers and social work assistants together worked with thirty people, or 60 per cent of the total. Specialists of all types, together with the team leader, worked with twenty people, or 40 per cent of the group.

It is apparently not a prerequisite for social workers to specialise in mental handicap, as most people in this study were on mixed case loads, where they were seen as social work "clients" alongside other individual clients and client groups. In a context of normalisation, this appears to be a logical development. Also, it may offer sensitive people some reassurance if they share the area office waiting room with clients other than people with mental handicaps. Social workers who are observed dealing with children, other adults, and elderly people might seem less threatening to them, than those known only to deal with people with mental handicaps.

Not surprisingly perhaps, the task of long-term support of the people in this study had aspects in common with provision of support to other social work clients in their own homes. Practical help and advice, personal support and counselling, emotional involvement and mediation, crisis intervention and group work skills, were all drawn more from generic social work principles and practices than from any specialist knowledge of mental handicap.

Frequency of contact	Research group	
	Number	Per cent
Weekly	29	58
Fortnightly	5	10
2 – 4 weeks	11	22
4 – 6 weeks	5	10
	50	100

TABLE 2. Frequency of social workers' contact with research group members

Research group members were seen regularly and often by their social workers (see Table 2). Twenty-nine people, or 58 per cent of the total, were seen every week, and six of these were seen more than once a week. The people who received this level of contact from their social workers were distributed between minimum support groups (nineteen out of twenty-six) and own homes (ten out of sixteen). None of the (eight) people living in family or institutional settings received this level of contact.

Thirty four people, or 60 per cent of the group, saw their social worker at least once in two weeks. Few people saw their social worker less than once a month, and three of the five who did were living in institutional settings.

Length of contact

The fourteen social workers working with research group members at the time of the study had been doing so for an average of 3.16 years. This is an extended period of time: a time long enough for trust to develop and confidence to grow on both sides; for the relaxation of formalities; and time, perhaps, for a move into friendship.

Length of contact ranged from six months to seven years. Two people had known their current social worker for only six months, though they knew their previous one for seven years. Another four had known their social worker for about a year. However, at the other end of the range, seven people had known their social worker for five years; five had known their social worker for six years; and a further four had known their current social workers for seven years.

The social work task

The minimum support group, as explained earlier, was Somerset Social Services Department's approved model of independent living. It was a "package deal", and part of the package was the allocated social worker. The departmental handbook entry reads thus: "The Group's social worker is the central coordinator of support giving, visiting at least once a week, dealing with problems as they arise". Further, it is stated that the social worker should: "help the members discover and use the facilities of the area, shops, services, places of entertainment, etc., make contact with neighbours, friends, relatives and clubs, all with a view to independent living".

In minimum support groups the social work task was specified; it was to make regular and frequent contact with people with a view to enabling them to lead independent lives within their local communities. It was, in fact, about all of life; about self-presentation and making friends; about leisure, pleasure, and structuring time; and about illness, loss, separation and, for some, about growing old.

For people living in their own homes the social work task was similarly global, embracing most aspects of daily life. These people were self-selected and may, therefore, have been well-motivated towards achieving independence. However, they shared with the people in minimum support groups an institutional background and a label of mental handicap; and their striving towards independence could lead them into difficulties. There was no "package deal" of structured support for them; and there was less control of their experimentation. In this context, people and their respective social workers each had to define the social work task in the light of individual needs and circumstances. This task might not remain static; it might change over time and, in the light of experience, might need to be renegotiated.

The social work task was complex. It had *formal* elements, such as practical and financial help, provision of services, mediation, crisis intervention, and personal support; and it had *informal* elements, the personal contact and personal feelings that developed in close and long-term relationships. One social worker described his role, in relation to Gerald Turner, in this way: "It's got several elements to it. I'm an official from the Social Services Department, and in that role I'm the rent collector and the person who handles official problems; I may discuss the garden, the fence that has blown down, the leaking roof, the plumbing, or operating the central heating system more efficiently, all the important household things. I'm also a friend. I'm not just a social worker; I'm something much broader than that, a whole load of things rolled into one".

For the purposes of analysis, the different elements of the social work task will be taken separately and examined in detail. This is an artificial separation. In practice, for example, discussion of personal problems may occur more easily and naturally when a social worker is engaged with someone in a practical activity, such as putting up curtains or laying a carpet. And all types of help are offered within the context of a relationship between two people, and the feelings that are engendered in both parties.

CHAPTER FIVE

The formal aspects of the social work task

The social worker's role

The formal aspects of the social worker's role comprised six elements: practical help; financial assistance; provision of (or referral to) services; mediation skills; crisis intervention; and personal advice and support. Each element will be taken in turn.

Practical help

Social workers were, in this study, expected to be practical people. Examples abound in the case notes, and in the testimonies of social workers and people with mental handicaps. The general maintenance of the home, and the comfort and appearance of the people who lived in it, were seen as key areas of concern. Thus, social workers were regularly engaged in discussing with people new or replacement items that were needed for the home; a new carpet or curtains, a new television or fridge freezer or automatic washing machine. Social workers and people living in the home discussed the options and went shopping together.

Similarly, new clothes and shoes, or personal items such as a tape recorder or record player, were selected on joint shopping expeditions. This was often one of the "fun things" of the social work task and brought the two parties into informal contact. As one social worker expressed it: "We make it a trip out, it's something special. It's doing things together".

Social workers were sometimes involved in repairs in the home. Some simple jobs were done personally, for example: running repairs to the fridge; fixing the curtain rail; soldering speakers: changing light bulbs; de-scaling the kettle; even, in one case, laying a concrete path ("That was beyond the call of duty!"). Sometimes social workers aimed to show people how to do small jobs so that they could do them independently in future, for example: how to wire a plug; how to work the thermostat; how to put up Christmas decorations and make a Christmas pudding; and how to sew trouser hems. Some enterprising people frequented secondhand shops in search of bargains, bringing home clocks, record players, radios, and fires which did not work. It appeared to be part of the social work task "to make things work!"

Most people were local authority tenants and were aware of the structural problems that should be referred to the local housing department. Many did this themselves, and obtained help for damp patches, leaking guttering, sticking doors, and faulty cisterns. Less confident people asked their social workers to intercede on their behalf. Either way, several social workers commented favourably on the good and fast service that people received from district council housing departments; a service better than that received by other client groups.

There were other aspects of practical help. Less simple repairs sometimes needed the attention of an electrician or a plumber, and the necessary arrangements had to be made. When redecorating the house or flat people were involved in choosing the paint and wall-paper. They often did some or most of the redecorating themselves, or else they helped the social worker and/or volunteers who were doing it with them. As some people grew older and frailer, they needed aids in the home; and social workers organised bath rails, second stair rails, and hand rails for the front path, for them.

There were two other major areas of practical help: dealing with correspondence; and coping with new situations. With regard to the first area some people could not read or write at all, and relied on their social workers to write letters for them and write birthday and Christmas cards to friends and family. In one situation Keith Gill, who was illiterate, needed the help of his social worker to choose an appropriate birthday card and write it for his wife, Beryl, who was literate and who *did* like to receive a card from him.

Some people did have some reading and writing ability and conducted their own correspondence with friends and family. However, everyone needed help in dealing with official correspondence, and this was a task carried out by social workers. Filling in DHSS forms and replying to DHSS letters of enquiry were the most common examples. Social workers gave other examples too: writing out a job application: applying for a housing transfer: applying for an allotment; booking a holiday; and completing the electoral form.

With regard to the second area, practical assistance was needed in helping people cope with complex situations outside the home. Many examples of this kind of help were reported, including:

registering with a new doctor, or going to the local dentist or chiropodist for the first time; taking the cat to visit the vet; going to the launderette for the first time; opening a building society account or a bank account; voting in local or national elections; making a will. Some people made a first attempt themselves to cope with a new and unfamiliar situation: often they succeeded if they met with sympathetic people who helped them; but sometimes they failed to complete the task and sought the social worker's help in a second attempt. Other people sought help in the first instance. Whether it was a first or subsequent attempt, the social worker's aim was the same; simply to show the person what to do and how to behave appropriately. They might talk about it first, and rehearse it, but essentially the learning took place in the real situation: the person carried out the transaction with the help of the social worker.

Most practical help given was necessary and welcomed. This aspect of his social worker's role was summed up by Edward Hayes, in the research interview: "If I have a complaint and ring him he'll come and sort it out. He comes now and again anyway. He has a look round, makes sure everything is all right, sees if we have any complaints, and has a chat".

Sometimes, however, practical "help" was seen as interference, and was not welcomed. Joan Woods and her two companions hoarded food and rubbish, to such an extent that their home presented a health hazard and was a fire risk. Part of the social worker's concern with the friends' health and wellbeing was expressed in the clearing out of hazardous materials. This was "practical help" in terms of the social work task, but it was regarded as an infringement of personal liberty, even theft, by Joan. One particularly grand clear-out got the social worker into "bad favour", and she commented thus: "They've never forgiven us. They say we took some of their things". Indeed, Joan referred to this herself in the research interview: "We found some of our papers were moved when we got home again. Some I haven't found to this day".

This was not the only instance in this study where well-intentioned, directive help, defined as such by the social worker, was perceived as interference by the recipient. In Joan Woods' case, battles over hoarded "rubbish" had a long history. No one had developed an entirely satisfactory way of equating concern for Joan's health and safety with her right to lead her own life. However, earlier entries in case notes from previous social workers did suggest that talking through the issues with her, and engaging her interest and involvement, worked better than direct and peremptory action.

Financial help

People living independently in the community were expected to be financially self-sufficient. Part of the "package deal" built into minimum support groups was a structure which controlled expenditure, encouraged savings, and monitored weekly individual and household finances. The social worker was a key person in this structure, though it also depended on the goodwill and cooperation of group members.

Each member of a minimum support group paid a weekly accommodation charge, part of which was a furnishing element. The combined contributions of a joint household were made available from central funds in the form of a cash grant, allocated each year. It was this grant which paid for replacement of furniture, furnishings, and equipment. The social worker's role, in this context, was to help people decide how to spend the money. This was usually straightforward and pleasurable, especially in the early years as people were building up comfortable and individualised homes. Later on, it sometimes became more difficult to make these decisions, and one social worker explained how he had to take in catalogues and make his own suggestions in order to kindle some interest. The people in his group had lived in their home for several years and, he said, "they genuinely feel they have enough of everything".

People in their own homes did not have this arrangement. Some, like Laura Vickers saved up for replacement items; some, like Keith and Beryl Gill, signed hire purchase agreements; others relied on the ingenuity of their social workers to find funds. Social workers were able to tap voluntary sources, and sometimes social services area funds or central funds. They helped people in their own homes to acquire a wide range of essential furniture and equipment, as well as televisions, washing machines, and hi-fi equipment.

Another area of social work involvement was in monitoring the weekly expenses of people living independently. Again there was a structure for people living in minimum support groups; certain amounts were set aside each week for accommodation, bills, and general housekeeping. Usually one person in the group took responsibility for collecting the set amounts from the others, and that person would then take the money into the social services area office or, alternatively, hand it over to the social worker during the weekly visit. Doreen Gilmore opted for the former system. She collected all her companions' money and sorted it out into set amounts. Then she returned some pocket money to each person and kept some for herself. She set aside money for the household kitty, television rental and licence money, lunch clubs, and the hairdresser. She then took the accommodation fees into the social services area office, to the social worker. She also took in any surplus money, and this was paid into a joint building society account.

Other people in minimum support groups collected the money in a similar fashion, but handed it over to the visiting social worker. Fiona Appleby followed a weekly "important ritual"; she collected the money from her companions, counted it out, and handed it over to the social worker. Similarly, Gerald Turner acted as "banker" in his group, handing over the requisite sum when his social worker called.

The system worked well for most groups. It left people with money in their pockets for personal spending, and for savings schemes. The area of personal finance, though much more private, could still involve the social worker. Dennis Adams' heavy commitment to his personal saving schemes led him to neglect paying rent and to building up arrears, a situation which inevitably led to conflict with his social worker. Ironically his companion, Roland Masters, used to spend every penny he received and he frequently had no savings for the television licence, or for Christmas, or for his annual holiday. His social worker commented: "He is very private about money and does not like to discuss it. He will not accept any help in devising savings plans".

A more unusual problem was someone with private means who did not like spending money. For example, Douglas Fields had private money administered by the Court of Protection and his social worker tried to persuade him to spend some of it. She explained her view: "He is over 60, and he can't take it with him. He goes round looking like a ragbag, and he lets Philip buy the drinks and pay for the taxis".

In people's own homes there was no comparable weekly monitoring system. In small one- and two-person units the household and personal finances were inextricably linked, and people had to find ways to make their fixed weekly income cover both areas. Some managed this feat remarkably well; for example, Laura Vickers and Geoffrey King were largely self-taught, successful home managers who only needed to discuss new, or particularly large, ventures with their social workers. Others, such as Agnes Cunningham and Olive Davis, and Bruce and Helen Winters, who used to live in minimum support groups, simply continued their old practice of putting set amounts to one side each week. Their social workers continued too their own established practice of calling each week to collect the money.

In some people's own homes, however, there were histories of financial problems and social work involvement in these. The people who sought financial autonomy seemed most at risk of financial difficulty. However, it was such a delicate and personal area that people often refused to discuss their finances at all, unless forced by dire circumstances to do so. Social workers had a difficult task. They were usually anxious to avoid financial chaos and wished to promote, instead, a budgeting system with built-in savings. Their advice, however, at best fell on deaf ears and at worst caused resentment.

Joan Woods, Mabel West, and Vera Bainbridge, for example, with all their additions and Joan's private means, brought in large sums of money each week. They kept large amounts in the house, paying cash for catalogue items and buying luxury goods from doorstep salesmen. At the same time, they were virtually housebound and were running up enormous fuel bills. Joan often made long telephone calls. Their social worker tried to talk about budgeting, to avoid the panic that occurred every time a large bill arrived; and had tried to discuss the dangers of keeping cash in the house. She explained her difficulties: "I've tried to help them to budget, but they don't want to know. Joan is very independent. I've tried to suggest that they put money into their Post Office account but they will not hear of it; they insist on keeping cash in the house. Joan simply will not discuss finances".

Ironically, bids for financial independence, if they failed, could actually increase people's dependency. Ralph and Enid Walker had learned this hard lesson, and so had Keith and Beryl Gill. Ralph and Enid had a history of rent arrears, threatened fuel disconnections, and cash crises necessitating loans and food parcels from the social worker. Their independence was eroded when their essential outgoings, their rent and fuel charges, were taken over by the DHSS. At the time of the study their social worker was trying to restore some financial responsibility back to them. She explained this: "I'm trying to encourage savings, that they think about tomorrow, not just today. I think management of their affairs is important to them, therefore I have encouraged them to re-start a Post Office account, and to take *responsibility* for it themselves. I'm trying to help them understand that it is through responsibility, through behaving responsibly, that they achieve their independence".

Similarly, Keith and Beryl Gill had a history of financial chaos. They had run up arrears and bills, begged cash loans on a variety of pretexts (lost purse, lost money, theft, and mugging).They had been bailed out with cash loans, small grants, and food parcels. Often they had made matters worse: for example, by Keith going off on drinking sprees and breaking into the gas meter; offences for which he received fines. They had signed hire purchase agreements beyond their means, and had had to visit the pawn shop. The social worker's comment, in the case notes, was as follows: "Ironically their bids to increase their independence fail so dismally that they are forever dependent on the Social Services Department to rectify their mistakes and to bail them out of cash crises. I try to advise them but they do not listen. They regard it as interference".

There seemed no easy way of acting as financial adviser in these instances, without undermining people's personal responsibility or invading their personal space. Yet *not* to act as financial advisor could, in the long run, bring about these outcomes anyway. The examples illustrate most vividly the delicate task of negotiating the boundaries between independence (with its attendant risks) and an acceptable level of advice giving and receiving. There was no formula. Social workers and service users had to work it out between them, not on a once-and-for-all basis but for a trial run, subject to review and renegotiation. There were no short-cuts.

Finally, some social workers were engaged in helping people manage their private means. Two had money tied up with the Court of Protection, and the social worker concerned dealt with official correspondence and withdrawals. Another had needed help in dealing with solicitor's fees. A fourth person, Laura Vickers, received a small annual income from Treasury Bonds and the social worker helped her to reclaim the tax deducted at source.

Provision of services
An element of the social work task was for social workers to act

as referring agents to obtain a particular service or form of help on behalf of service users. Six forms of help of this kind were found in the study: the seeking of a daytime placement; the introduction of people to a new leisure activity; the recruitment of volunteers to teach a particular skill; the recruitment of volunteers to befriend people; the referral of people for medical or psychiatric help; and, when all else failed, the referral of people to an alternative residential setting.

Many people in the study attended daytime placements; the local training centre, a social club, the Red Cross Club, a lunch club, or an elderly persons' home. These placements were found for them by their social workers. Thus Charles Deacon, for example, was referred for part-time attendance at the local training centre by his social worker who felt that he needed company outside the home, a place he could use as "a social club" for meeting people. And Joyce Hardcastle was referred for day care at an elderly persons' home because the social worker noted her "erratic behaviour, temper tantrums, and crying fits at home". Both placements were successful. Over seven years later Charles still attended the centre, and Joyce, in her social worker's words, "feels important at the elderly persons' home; she has the sort of status there she needs to offset her very limited role at home".

Similarly some people were referred, or introduced, to leisure settings. Many people first joined their local Gateway Club through introductions by social workers. Others, like Iris Barber, were introduced to adult literacy classes at the local college of further education; or, like Arthur Stott, to local art classes; or, like Martin Forest and Howard Bell, to pottery classes in the local adult education college.

Sometimes volunteers were found to visit the home, to assist in a particular project or to teach a new skill. Several people were visited by adult literacy tutors. Others had been helped with gardening, sometimes in a rescue bid to dig up, or rotovate, a particularly difficult or neglected area; and sometimes on a longer-term basis, to help people plan a more creative use of land. Other volunteers had come to improve cooking skills; to teach Edgar Carter how to bake better cakes, and Doreen Gilmore how to apply herself to imaginative and creative cookery. A more unusual volunteer was needed for the group which bought a Monopoly game and could not understand the rules; an 'A' level economics student played it with them. As a result group members learned a new skill, and an extended vocabulary of phrases such as "getting a mortgage" and "going bankrupt".

People thought by social workers to be lonely were put in touch with volunteers to befriend them. For example, a volunteer was found to befriend Glenda Potts on the following grounds: "She needs a mother figure; she has no relatives and needs someone to take her under their wing". Similarly Geoffrey King's social worker found him a volunteer to provide "company, conversation and companionship" on the grounds that: "He feels very lonely. He does not have much experience in making friends, nor any confidence in that direction".

Sometimes people were referred for medical help. For example, Mabel West, in failing physical and mental health, was referred to a geriatrician. Colin Markham was referred to his general practitioner for a thorough check up: "He complains of continually suffering from diarrhea. He does not always reach the toilet and the others always have to clear up after him. He is also lethargic, apathetic and is eating less and less. There is a fairly high level of concern about him at home". And Duncan Swales was referred to a psychiatrist, because his behaviour within the group was becoming more and more difficult for his companions to cope with. The referral letter listed five areas of concern: Duncan rarely went to bed, sleeping instead in the armchair by the electric fire; he was "very greedy" and raided the fridge and larder during the night, consuming huge quantities of food; he was a heavy smoker, becoming aggressive when he had no money left for cigarettes; he was a "compulsive spender", spending money on "unnecessary items"; and he had acquired a small hurricane lamp to warm the outside toilet pipes, and was buying meths and paraffin, thereby creating a potential fire risk.

Part of the social work task was, where appropriate, to seek an alternative placement for people who were so unhappy in their current situation that they were causing worry or unhappiness to those around them. Thus Glenda Potts and Denise Parker were found places in mental handicap hostels, and Bernard Chivers was found a place in an elderly persons' home.

Entries in Bernard's case notes referred to his tantrums and to him throwing articles of furniture around at midnight when he ran out of cigarettes. They continued: "when walking along the road, he mutters now almost continually to himself, and loud enough for passers-by to wonder whether he is speaking to them". Bernard settled well in his new environment, and his social worker reported: "There are now *no* problems". In no sense was the move seen as a failure, but as an appropriate move: "They adore him in there", and, "He simply loves it!". The social worker explained the change: "In the group he didn't want to be responsible for anything. He didn't want to be told what to do – he'd had enough of that kind of living. He wanted to lead his life the way he wanted to lead it. He wasn't free in that community. The more everyone got at him the worse he became. He began to lose his sense of identity, he had no structure or purpose to his day. It's very different now, the move to the home has helped his identity crisis. Being so much younger and so much more agile, he's able to rush around, get out the walking frames, run errands, go to the shops. He's a very useful member of that community – quite the opposite! And its coming *voluntarily* from him, he's giving out, he's making a contribution. And it's rebounding on him, he seems years younger".

Mediation skills

Sometimes people found themselves in difficulties with neighbours or shopkeepers, and social workers had to intervene to help both sides understand the problem and to smoothe over it. On some occasions it was the neighbour or the shopkeeper who contacted the social worker for assistance; at other times it was the indignant service user who sought an intermediary.

Several examples are given by social workers of occasions when neighbours sought help. Some "problems" were very minor, and were very easily resolved. For example, Charles Deacon's neighbours were concerned because members of the group were wandering around the house at night with lights on and curtains not drawn. The group only needed telling once about drawing their curtains; they were horrified to think people had seen them undressed.

Ada and Vincent Smith's neighbours complained in the early days of their new tenancy that they were nuisances; pestering people, knocking on doors, "scrounging", and chatting to visitors. The social worker invited someone round from the council, pointing out to him: "They are just a nice harmless old couple, trying to survive". He agreed, replied to the neighbours accordingly, and the complaints ceased.

The weekend he moved into his single person flat, Alan Perkins overloaded the electrical circuit, managing to fuse all the lights in the block and put all the television sets out of action. His social worker was called in to remonstrate: "He was so worried, he hid in the bathroom. I knew he was there. He was too frightened to come out. That was right at the beginning and we sorted it out. And now, they've taken him to their hearts".

Arthur Stott soon found himself in difficulty with a neighbour through the best of intentions. An ardent churchgoer, he listened intently to sermons and one night was particularly impressed with the vicar's text of "Love thy neighbour". He made a very literal interpretation of the sermon and hurried off to call on a local elderly widow living alone. It was a dark winter evening, she did not know Arthur, and she was alarmed by his unexpected appearance at her door. The social worker easily smoothed over the misunderstanding, and peace was restored.

Most of the reported difficulties occurred in the early days of people's move to the community, or transfer to a new home in a new area. Usually as they began to get to know their neighbours and the local shopkeepers, difficulties were resolved directly between the parties concerned. The role of the social worker as mediator appeared to characterise the early stages of community living.

The few recorded and recalled difficulties involving shopkeepers were quite trivial. A butcher telephoned, expressing concern about the size of the bills two people were running up in his shop. Another shopkeeper telephoned the social worker when Geoffrey King lost his temper and swore at the girl shop assistant. And a pub landlord grew concerned because every night, at the busiest time, Daniel Baxter would come in with seven small orders and seven (incorrect) amounts of money, and would take up half-an-hour of prime drinking time negotiating his way through his list.

Sometimes people asked the social worker for help as an intermediary, usually when their own tactics had not worked. Thus Dennis Adams and Roland Masters sought help in dealing with local children who were teasing them by knocking on their door and running away. The social worker enlisted the support of near neighbours who successfully saw off the offending children. Geoffrey King sought his social worker's help in complaining about neighbours who had made complaints about him. Robert Harper asked his social worker to speak firmly to the home help who picked his prize strawberries, and Keith Gill brought in his social worker to resolve a dispute with his landlady.

People rarely complained about shopkeepers: if they ran into difficulty it seemed that they simply steered clear of the offending person in future. No instances were recorded or recalled; except for two sub-postmasters who caused a great deal of distress by refusing to accept Colin Markham's mark and Grace Lister's block capitals as valid signatures. Grace was quite distraught; this happened in a busy post office on her first visit and she felt publicly humiliated. The social worker intervened, first with a friendly telephone call, and then with a formal letter to the Area Manager of the Post Office. Grace received an apology and her signature was accepted.

The relatively few examples of this kind of help being needed suggest that people learned quickly from their early experiences how to get along with neighbours, and which shops to patronise and which to avoid. They learned who were the kindly neighbours and who were the helpful shopkeepers, and they built these people into their support networks. Social workers were rarely called in as mediators; if they were, the minor misunderstandings were quickly resolved.

Crisis intervention

The term "crisis" is here taken to mean an event which requires urgent action. This is to isolate those occurrences which require an immediate response from those which, though pressing and possibly "critical" for an individual, can be handled by more conventional means. People in the research group experienced relatively few crises of this sort, though a few were recalled or recorded. There were some examples: four fires; injuries through accidents or falls; the onset of severe illness; and the deaths of four people, two of these at home.

On most of these occasions the person concerned, with the help of his or her support network, coped with the crisis. Perhaps the essential part of the social work task in this context was to ensure that people knew what to do and whom to contact in an emergency, and that they had people nearby on whom they could call. This seemed to be the system which operated effectively for the people in this study; in an emergency they coped and the social worker was not usually called in. Indeed, the social worker might not hear about the crisis until the next day, or, perhaps, not until the next visit.

Joan Woods, in the research interview, described a fire of two years previously. "I was cooking tea, I had the grill on and someone came to the door. I left the grill on and went to talk to the neighbour. The tea towel on the oven door caught fire and we had to send for the Fire Brigade". On another occasion, in the same household, elderly Vera Bainbridge had a bad fall at 12.30am: "She lay on the floor in a pool of blood". Again Joan acted decisively and appropriately; she telephoned her family doctor and called him out to attend to Vera.

It seemed that people knew when to seek immediate help. If they were too frightened to summon help themselves they might run to a kind neighbour. For example, a group's television set caught fire one evening when three people were watching it and the fourth was upstairs having a bath. Doreen Gilmore switched the set off and pulled out the plug, and she and Arthur Stott ran off to different neighbours to seek help. The fire was successfully extinguished by the neighbours, but everyone was in a state. Three people were "obviously shaken" and the fourth, abandoned in his bath, was "hysterical"; also the cat had gone berserk. All four, and the cat, were taken to the neighbour's house to recover themselves.

In situations of this kind the social worker often came in, after the event, to help the participants sort out the longer-term issues. One fire was caused when a group used a paraffin heater following the breakdown of their gas boiler; the social worker ensured that the Gas Board fixed the boiler as a matter of urgency. After Joan Wood's fire, the social worker arranged for Joan and her elderly companions to spend a few days in an elderly persons' home, allowing time to put the house right, instal a new cooker, and re-decorate the kitchen. Laura Vickers coped with Gordon's heart attack by running to a neighbour's flat; but she needed the social worker's assistance afterwards to cope with her bereavement and help her attend to all the formalities attached to her husband's death. And Rita Young's social worker, after Rita's spectacular breakdown in her minimum support group, afterwards helped her to "rebuild her shattered life".

A rather different sort of crisis was the internal crisis; conflict within the group. This situation posed severe problems for the participants. It was seen as a very private matter, certainly not one to share with neighbours and acquaintances. Initially it seemed it was not an issue to share with anybody, as admitting to internal dissension was seen as tantamount to admitting failure. Social workers, as authority figures, might not be told for a long time about dissent within a group; it was a private, domestic matter and all participants, including the victim, hushed up the matter. One social worker described his experience of this tendency as follows: "It's based on their institutional background. Group members show loyalty by not splitting on one another. It's a kind of collective paranoia towards authority".

If a situation at home was particularly difficult, then signs of tensions or distress would eventually show despite loyalty or collective paranoia. Sometimes the victim would eventually break down in tears and confess all to the social worker, as happened with Joyce Hardcastle. On other occasions the victim would walk into the day centre sporting a black eye, as happened to Elaine Court when neither she, nor her companions, could give a convincing explanation of how this injury had occurred. The tears, or the black eye, signalled the end of the silent phase; the conflict was then out in the open. When participants found that verbal, even physical, aggression at home did not automatically mean return to hospital, then the dissent could be discussed. In such circumstances social workers were seen as appropriate people in whom to confide and they were called in, or telephoned, during a conflict (which could last several days) or immediately afterwards, in order to help people understand and resolve their differences.

These conflicts were crises, and the violent feelings aroused could be very frightening. There was no simple recourse to a kind neighbour or the emergency services. It was in the context of severe intra-group dissent that social workers were most likely to use their skills of crisis intervention. One social worker recalled the domestic situation in one group home: "The situation was explosive, there was evidence of tears and violence. They called me in to restore order". The scene in another group home was described to the social worker afterwards by a relative who witnessed it: "Alan had already punched Melanie in the face ... he was in a dangerous mood ... the two boys were terrified and Melanie was crying and would not come downstairs ...".

The social work task, as seen by social workers, was first to restore order in a frightening situation, and then to help the participants understand their differences. One social worker explained how she was "called into domestic disputes which get out of hand" and had to calm the situation down by her presence at the scene: "There is a good deal of trust and they will listen, eventually". Another social worker described the "emotional tensions" of his group; and the several occasions on which he was called in to deal with "the breakdown of interpersonal relationships": "I tried each time to sort it out, explain it, smoothe it over". And a third social worker described the "internal crises" of her group, and her interventions in these, while seeking "to disentangle the threads of their conflicts, to help them understand what goes wrong".

If the first phase of such conflict was silence, and the second phase was crisis intervention, then the next phase was resolution. The social work task was to help people to live amicably together. It was often possible, when differences had been aired and understood, for people to continue living together. However, in several groups in this study, differences between people had led to changes in group membership. Several people moved out of groups into a marital home or their own home; and other people moved into family placements or institutional settings. An essential part of the social work task was this positive resolution of domestic crises. Those who *chose* to leave, and those who *had* to leave, were all people who left minimum support groups with the help of their social workers. In every instance the move was seen by both parties as a positive move. Groups shedding a "difficult" fourth person tended not to replace that person with another member; and found that their differences ceased.

Domestic crises of this sort were confined to people living in groups. The interpersonal difficulties that occurred in people's own homes did not, at least in this study, reach crisis level. The social worker picked these up and dealt with them in the ordinary course of regular contact with the people concerned.

Personal advice and support

This was an area of the research rich in examples. It was a key element in the social work task. All the people in the study had talked to their own social workers about some areas of concern. These were not group, or household, issues; they were areas of private concern. In this context, people turned to social workers as to a personal counsellor or confidante.

There seemed to be five main spheres of concern for people: relationships; loss; status; personal presentation; and future plans.

Relationships

Geoffrey King had problems in making friends; yet he was lonely and would have liked companions, preferably to get married. He discussed this problem every week with his social worker. An entry in the case notes reads: "Every week we do a total review of his current life situation in the context, at his insistence, of all that has gone before. Thus we try to understand the past; his family rejection, his ambivalent relationship with his aunt . . . ". Geoffrey actively sought some insight into his problems in trusting people.

The whole area of personal feelings, of coping with emotional reactions in themselves and others, was an area of concern for social workers and service users. For example, Joyce Hardcastle loved to tease people, particularly Arthur Stott, even though it almost invariably led to trouble and tears. Her social worker tried to "calm, comfort and reassure her . . . and help her to understand what it is she does . . . try to modify her behaviour . . .". Rita Young was racked by self-doubt and uncertainty, and her social worker recorded her efforts to help Rita gain in confidence and security: "I offer a great deal of support and reassurance, and give her encouragement, to build up her self-confidence and her belief in her own abilities to cope". Rita's feelings of worthlessness affected her ability to make and maintain friendships.

Robert Harper needed his social worker's help in coming to terms with his feelings of jealousy when two of his friends were developing a close relationship, and excluding himself and another friend. His feelings were so strong that he broke his twenty-nine years of self-imposed silence that had been in force since his earliest days in hospital. His social worker was the first person to hear him speak, and she recalled the occasion vividly: "He met me at the door and said 'Edgar's showing off in front of Norma. You come and sort him out!' Those were the first words he ever spoke to me. I didn't quite know how to react in those circumstances, but I ignored the fact that he had spoken. I didn't make an issue out of it. I said we'd better go in and talk about it". This was a major breakthrough in their relationship and in Robert's personal development, and he and his social worker began to have normal conversations. However, Robert still did not speak to past social workers, anyone attached to the hospital, or even the staff of the pub where he worked: "they belong to the silent past, the wrong era" (social worker).

Engagement, marriage, sex, and marital issues were areas discussed between people and their social workers. Charles Deacon discussed his possible engagement to Fiona Appleby, and Dennis Adams discussed his engagement to Kate Fowler in terms of finance, accommodation, and feelings. Sometimes the discussion of sex could prove difficult, as Edgar Carter's social worker discovered: "It was very hard to talk about it. Edgar's response was, 'Oh, that's wicked. I wouldn't think of such a thing. How could you think that I would do that!'". It was only after Gordon Vicker's death that Laura confided in her social worker that she had refused all his sexual overtures. She was quite matter of fact about it: "I done 50 years for the last time, I wasn't taking no chances". Ralph and Enid Walker ran into a stormy patch in their marriage when it seemed that Enid was having an affair with another man. It was a difficult time, and they both looked to their social worker to help them resolve their problems.

Loss

Many people had been forced to cope with loss in one form or another, and had looked to their social workers to support them through it. Charles Deacon, Robert Harper, Beryl Gill, and Fiona Appleby had suffered parental deaths; Cliff Dawson the death of a brother; and Laura Vickers the death of her husband. Enid Walker still grieved for the loss of her baby several years previously, and talked about her feelings with her social worker: "We have ongoing talks about the baby she lost. Seeing a young baby in the office brings back the memory, the sadness".

Loss of a key person through rejection was difficult for people to cope with, and again they needed support to come to terms with it. Cliff Dawson used to go to bingo with his sister until she abruptly stopped it; it seemed that she felt awkward being seen with him. Cliff was very hurt by this, and needed comfort. Nigel Short's social worker tried to make contact with his mother who lived locally, but she wrote back: "I wish to be left alone". Denise Parker's personal attempts to re-establish contact with her mother led to total rejection and great personal sadness. And Laura Vickers lived through the double trauma of her middle-aged adopted daughter returning to her life and, just as abruptly, disappearing from it again.

People kept pets. They indulged them with food, comfort, and privileges. They nursed them, played with them, walked with them, even painted them in their pictures of home. The loss of a pet was a very sad occasion. Maurice Dean began his grieving at the onset of illness, as his social worker described: "It's his sort of crisis. He thinks more of animals than of people. He breaks into floods of tears when his cat is ill, he breaks his heart. And when his cat died, his grief was uncontrollable – he was quite inconsolable".

Status

The two main areas of concern in this context were unemployment and retirement. Several men in the study were unhappy with their unemployed status. For example, Keith Gill had made valiant efforts to find work, but without success. His social worker expressed a great deal of concern for his plight: "He gets really upset that he can't find a job. He feels less than a man, it's a hard pill to swallow. He is very defensive, very tender, very vulnerable. He recognises too well his own inadequacies". Dennis Adams had tried every pub in town looking for work; and Geoffrey King discussed his employment prospects every week with his social worker.

The subject of retirement was an area of some concern. It was seen as a milestone in life, a social acknowledgement of growing old and a reminder of mortality. Martin Forest became very anxious when he reached retirement age; he was concerned about ageing and the implications for his future. Where would he live? Would he have to move? He needed a great deal of reassurance that life would continue in much the same way and that his present home would continue to be his home. Mabel West's social worker helped her, and her two companions, when they retired from the local training centre. He thought that he had successfully worked through their strong feelings about retirement, and that they had accepted their new status. However, a seven-page letter written by Mabel, and signed by all three, clearly showed they had *not* accepted their status as retired people, and that much more work was needed. Mabel wrote: "I shall never like being on my retirement, no I don't like it at all, nor Joan or Vera, we don't like it at all ... I don't believe in retirement ... is there any need of us to retire ... now we'll be lost not coming any more . . . . From one of your unhappy, once a very happy but now unhappy, Mabel, Joan, Vera".

Personal presentation

It was a straightforward situation when someone recognised a need to improve his or her personal appearance, or to improve the house, or to behave in socially acceptable ways. These were very personal matters, but service users and their social workers did discuss them and took appropriate steps. This kind of social work help, where people saw the need for change, was more in the province of practical help. Social workers and service users planned their strategy and went together to the shops, the dentist, or the hairdresser; they acquired the services of a home help or volunteer; or practised social skills together.

Sometimes, however, someone's appearance, hygiene, or behaviour was a matter of concern to others; to companions or neighbours perhaps. Similarly, there were occasions when one person's standards of housekeeping fell short of other people's expectations. The state of the house might then cause concern, not to that person, but to others who had to live in it, or visit it, or live next door to it. Social workers were faced then with a valid area of concern; but "personal advice and support" in this context was sometimes regarded as interference or infringement of rights by the person who was taken to task.

Ada and Vincent Smith's social worker was concerned about their personal hygiene. She could smell them, but they were unaware of this: "It's a difficult subject. I tried asking them if they had any difficulty bathing, if they would like a bath nurse or bath aids, but they said no, they didn't. They resent any interference of any sort which might suggest that they are not managing. It's difficult to give them advice unless they bring up a subject themselves that they are worried about". Similarly, Geoffrey King and Alan Perkins were careless of their appearance and personal hygiene but did not welcome interference on the subject.

Alan Perkins' home was of some concern too. He cluttered his minimum support group with piles of his collected items; later his single-person flat was piled high "with dozens of trays of plant cuttings, empty packets, paper bags ... tons of rubbish". His social worker was concerned, but her advice was not welcomed. Joan Woods, too, had battled with a succession of social workers in her determination to maintain her home in its current state. She too saw advice, in this context, as interference.

Sometimes, in the early days of living in the community, people had to learn about socially acceptable ways of behaving; and often it was the social worker who had to offer advice on the subject. Geoffrey King's midnight jaunts attracted the attention of the police; Elaine Court's constant invitations to tea wearied the local shopkeeper; Daniel Baxter's neighbours listened with horror to his lurid accounts of happenings at home; and Pamela Mercer burdened her local pub landlord with her confidences even when the pub was closed. It seemed that advice on behaviour in the community was acceptable, and was heeded; and social workers noted that such incidents ceased on being discussed.

Future plans

People did not necessarily see themselves continuing to live in the same situation indefinitely. They looked ahead to a different future, and engaged their social workers in discussing their plans.

Alice Wise, for example, had lived for several years in a minimum support group, but at the time of the follow-up was living in a family placement. She saw this as a temporary measure, a half-way stage between group home and independence. She explained in the research interview how she discussed her future plans with her social worker: "Mrs. Fisher is my social worker now. She don't worry me. She's nice to talk to. We talk about all sorts of things, like getting my own place. I want a little house so I can be independent. I've got sheets, bath towels, tea cloths, cups and saucers, knives and forks, tins of fruit, and tea in the loft, ready for when I move".

Similarly, Edward Hayes had plans for his future too, but he was not receiving a very sympathetic hearing from his social worker. He explained his plans, and his social worker's reaction, in the research interview: "I been thinking for a long time, I'd like a move. Mr. Hill don't hold with that one. I don't know why. I'd like my own house, one bedroom, one up one down. We can't agree".

Views of research group members

It was clear from the testimony they gave just who members of the research group would turn to in difficulty, as all the people interviewed talked about their social workers in this context. All had sought help in the past with their problems, and anticipated seeking help again when in difficulty. Even people who expressed some ambivalent or negative feelings about their social workers still saw them as "someone to turn to" for help.

People readily gave examples of how their social workers had helped or had failed to help them. Some quotes from interviews with service users illustrate both the range of social work activity as seen through their eyes, and their evaluation of that activity.

Some positive comments

Douglas Fields   "We are going on holiday in August. Mrs. Morley is arranging it. She helped us stuff our Christmas turkey too."

Melanie Saunders	(same minimum support group; same social worker). "I go to *Safeways* every Friday with Daphne. She came round this morning to show me how to cook a pizza for dinner."
Bruce Winters	"Mrs. Hayes collects our money, buys chairs and things when we need new ones and fixes the telly. She has our names down for a bungalow so we don't have to worry about stairs.
	We've got a phone but we can't use it. My wife doesn't understand numbers, and I get the wrong number every time. Mrs. Hayes is going to get a press-button phone so we can ring her up. She rings us up. I answer it, and tell her how we are."
Ada Smith	"Mrs. Lewis calls now and then. She helps us get clothes and fixes our holidays. Mr. Carter used to be our social worker, but we're not under him now. He calls us friends. We're under Mrs. Lewis now."
Maurice Dean	"Mr. Taylor is my social worker now. He took me in his car to buy a new telly. I'm going to ask him if I can see my (hospital) records, but I don't know if we're allowed to or not."
Agnes Cunningham	"Mr. Williams does a lot for us. He sorts our money out. He's finding a home for my dad – he's 91. He takes Olive to her sister's for her holidays. He looks after her pension book while she's away."
Bridget Cook	"Mrs. Brooks is the only visitor I get at home. She's very good to me. She takes me in her car to stay with my mum and dad on the farm."
Carol Hart	"Patrick helped me find a job. He's arranging for me to go swimming on Sunday mornings with a lady from our village."
Denise Parker	"Peter is going to find out about my brother. He lives at North Cross, I think,

| | but I don't know his number. Peter will find him, when he's not too busy." |
| *Glenda Potts* | "Cathy is my social worker now. She came to see me on Thursday, and I'll see her again at the centre on Monday. I like her, she's nice. She's arranged for me to go on holiday to Weston-Super-Mare with two friends." |

Some negative comments

Ralph Walker	"One thing gets me, Lesley (volunteer) and Theresa (social worker) pass me from one to the other, so I don't know where I am. I ask Lesley something, and she'll say 'You have to ask Theresa'. Then if I ask Theresa, she'll say, 'Well what does Lesley think?'"
Joan Woods	"Mrs. Pearce comes sometimes, not very often. I suppose she is my social worker? She only took over temporary. She hasn't helped me with very much actually. She hasn't helped find Mabel's savings book, or done that bit of garden at the front. She hasn't done a jolly scrap!"
Geoffrey King	"The social worker helps me in some ways – like I have a roof over my head, and clothes to wear. But she doesn't make my life happy. She doesn't sort my life out. She hasn't got me a job, or got me some friends – the important things in life."

The range of social work activity, as described by service users, was wide and varied. People readily gave examples of practical help, such as arranging holidays, assisting with shopping and cooking, and replacing a traditional unusable telephone with a push button version. Social workers were valued too for their involvement in people's social lives; for making links with family and friends, for extending social contacts, and for being "nice" people to have around.

Negative comments here were more reflections on what social workers failed to do than on their propensity to interefere in people's lives. The underlying suggestion from everyone making criticisms was that social workers could and should do more. Some ideas were practical (helping with the garden and finding a savings book) but others were to do with personal style and the nature of the social work task. Ralph Walker looked for a more direct and honest approach. Geoffrey King looked for changes in his life: help in finding a job and making friends.

CHAPTER SIX

The informal aspects of the social work task

The social worker's role

The social work task was characterised by informality. This may not seem surprising as the work covered many fundamental aspects of people's lives, and took place within long-term relationships which involved frequent and regular contact.

Many people had their social worker's home address and/or telephone number. The latter was particularly important, even if it was rarely used. Gerald Turner's social worker had explained that it was for emergencies only, and Gerald respected this. Charles Deacon was able to telephone his previous social worker when the television set went wrong and the central heating system failed. Laura Vickers would ring her social worker for a chat, or to let her know when something nice had happened: "I thought you would like to know, dear".

All social workers called the people with whom they worked by their first names, and many service users reciprocated. It was not a universal practice, however, and many service users continued to use a formal address. There was not necessarily any other overt observation of formal roles, and other expressions of informality sometimes accompanied such formal address. Households were sometimes divided in the use of names. Melanie Saunders addressed her social worker by her first name but her companions, Douglas Fields and Philip Grey, addressed her formally. Similarly, Cliff Dawson used his social worker's first name but his three companions opted for formal address. It appeared to be very much an individual arrangement, a personal preference.

It was shown earlier that social workers and service users were often engaged in doing things together; this might bring into the interaction an element of informality. Dennis Adams and Roland Masters used to go on shopping trips to a nearby city with their social worker, the day made special by morning coffee in a smart café and lunch in a pub. Philip Grey's social worker recalled their joint trip to do some Christmas shopping: "Philip said, 'When we get back we'll have a cup of tea.' It was so normal. We put all our shopping down, and he made the tea, and we had mince pies. And his face – it was absolutely glowing". Melanie Saunders used to take her social worker with her to buy new underclothes; requiring her to join her in the changing room to help her to struggle into her corsets. It was, undoubtedly, difficult to avoid informality in such transactions!

Social workers visits were often seen as a social occasion, a time to make tea and relax. If the visits were regular and predicted the kettle might be boiled in advance of the social worker's arrival. Many people provided hospitality: Howard Bell and Martin Forest would get out the tea and biscuits, though some weeks Howard baked a cake instead; Bruce and Helen Winters provided tea and cake. The ritual of hospitality guaranteed a minimum period of contact. It ensured that the social worker had to sit down, and be prepared to talk, for at least as long as it took for the tea to be prepared and consumed.

Often social workers were viewed as people to tell things to; especially the nice things that happened. In the visit following the breaking of his 29-year-long silence, Robert again met his social worker at the door: "He wanted to tell me all about their weekend away, what a marvellous time they'd had, the lovely food and the fun. Now he shares all his pleasures and joys!" Pamela Mercer also liked to share her pleasures; her new coat perhaps, or news about her family, or pictures of her boyfriend. Beryl Gill's social worker commented on Beryl's wish to share nice things: "She is keen to share her pleasures and joys, she loves me to take an interest. She is naïve and feels great excitement at simple things, like the cat's newest trick. I love her naïvety, she bubbles over with excitement, and that's good to watch, really good to see!"

The informality and the sharing of pleasure and joys sometimes led naturally to physical displays of affection. Helen Winters would greet her social worker at the door with a big hug, and Laura Vickers always said goodbye to hers with a hug and a kiss. Melanie Saunders' social worker commented: "She likes to hug and be hugged. She so obviously asks for love that I hug her when I would not hug other people. It must be lovely to have that personality, the warmth is so obviously there and it brings out the warmth in other people. You want to cuddle her and make a fuss of her, and I imagine everyone down the line who has dealt with her will have treated her like that".

Sometimes physical contact was for comfort, as well as an expression of affection. Olive Davis's social worker explained: "If I go there and Olive is upset, Agnes will say 'Olive is upset'. It's usually trivial, but I put my arm around her and give her a cuddle. She'll have a good cry, and feel better about it".

Social workers became involved in the special occasions in people's lives. Howard Bell and Martin Forest held birthday parties and invited their social worker; Bruce and Helen Winters' social worker was invited to birthday teas; and Laura Vickers was taken out to lunch by her social worker on her birthday. Christmas was a special time, and social workers were involved in buying trees, putting up decorations, making puddings, and delivering Christmas hampers. Gerald Turner, Eric Hastings, and Iris Barker saw their social worker on Christmas day when he called at their house to have sherry with them.

Holidays were important too, and social workers helped people make bookings. Sometimes they provided transport, as did Edgar Carter, Robert Harper, and Norma Jones's social worker when they went to stay in a holiday camp for the first time: "I hadn't much time that day and I had to leave them to sort themselves out. I felt some anxiety leaving them there, looking lost, not knowing which chalet was theirs. I need not have worried! When I arrived to pick them up I was greeted by the gateman who said, 'You must be Mrs.Brooks!' They had told him all about me — and not just him, but all the chalet maids. The whole camp knew about me and my arrival! They all said how much they had enjoyed having them, and everyone waved us off".

The informality of much of the social work contact led, in many situations, to a great deal of interest in, and concern about, the social worker as a person. The contact moved beyond social worker and client roles. Birthday cards were exchanged, and Christmas cards were sent. Holiday postcards were reciprocated. Helen Winters' social worker commented: "She always asks after my cat and family, and buys presents at holiday times and at Christmas". Edgar Carter baked cakes for his social worker to take home to her family. He even filled in football pools in her name: "The first I knew of this was when I had a win!" Olive Davis and Agnes Cunningham visited their social worker's wife in hospital: "They sat by the bed for half-an-hour, making conversation".

A very special treat for people was to be invited to their social worker's home, and several social workers had issued this invitation. For example, Doreen Gilmore, Joyce Hardcastle, Nigel Short, and Arthur Stott were always invited for lunch around Christmas. The social worker commented: "I noticed particularly how much at ease they were, yet it's not something they do that often ... Arthur was very much at ease, he had all the social graces. For example, he made conversation, stayed chatting for a while after eating, and then helped clear everything away".

Some social workers had left or changed their jobs, but still continued to see the people with whom they had worked. They were then regarded as friends. Edgar Carter maintained telephone contact and reciprocated social visits with two of his previous social workers. They also exchanged birthday cards and presents. Similarly, Ada and Vincent Smith maintained contact with three previous social workers. Their current social worker explained: "They don't see them as social workers ... they are friends, it's more of a friendship. They simply don't expect to be cut off". Again, telephone calls and social visits were continued.

The informality in the social work contact was striking. The social work task was so all-embracing that it transcended formal boundaries. The doing of things together, the sharing of pleasure and pain, the personal involvement in major life changes; all the formal elements of the social work role were carried out in the context of informality. Service users contributed much to this process. They were usually described with warmth and affection by their social workers, and their lack of inhibition and their openness was often commended.

Views of research group members

The choice of words, or mode of expression, varied between people, as the examples below illustrate. The unifying theme, however, was their perception of social workers as people, rather than of their formal role.

Charles Deacon   "We think Paul should come sooner on Mondays so he gets home to his family sooner. It's a long drive, more than 20 miles. We don't like to think of him getting home so late."

Joyce Hardcastle (in a letter to her social worker). "My Dear Friend ... I am thinking about you every day and night ... lots of love from your friend Joyce." (In interview) "Barbara is my friend. I get a present from her on my birthday."

Edgar Carter   "We're going to have a bit of fun with her. I'll ring her up, tell her to come over quick cos we can't get the hedgehog out!" (a new soft toy). "She'll laugh! You won't get anyone better, she's too good."

Laura Vickers   (in a letter to her social worker). "Dear friend, when are you coming back as I miss you quite a lot ... hope to hear soon. I hope it won't be long before I see you ... with love, Laura."

Beryl Gill   "The last holiday I had was a weekend away with Judy" (previous social worker). "Now it's Theresa who comes round. She sometimes calls at dinner time. If I'm cooking chips she'll take one."

Maurice Dean   "Mrs. Hart used to take us all out in the car, for rides to see different places. That was when I lived in the group. She died later, after I'd moved here on my own. I'm still a friend of her family though. I'm going to her daughter's wedding party on Saturday."

The imagery used by people in these descriptions captures nicely the informality of the social work task. It's expressed in terms of friendships, fun, car rides, holidays (together), and presents ...

CHAPTER SEVEN

Relationships between social workers and service users

Types of relationship

The social worker-service user relationships in this study were long-term. They were characterised by regular and frequent contact. They embraced practical and personal issues in formal and informal ways. Real feelings were evoked on both sides, often positive but occasionally negative.

The source of the descriptive material in this chapter was the research interviews with social workers. Part of each interview was focused on day-to-day events in service users' lives, but part of it was open-ended. Social workers were asked to think about, and describe, their own relationships with the people with whom they worked. All the information was collected "first hand" in this way; this was not the sort of comment noted by previous social workers in case notes.

The relationships described seemed to cluster into six types. The social worker was, or was seen as, a business contact, an informal official, the "big gun", a threat, a friend, or a close tie.

The social worker as a business contact

Alan Perkins' social worker described theirs as a "business relationship". She explained this: "If I went tomorrow, and someone else took over he wouldn't worry. I could be anybody. I'm just a support figure who is replaceable".

Similarly, Ada Smith's social worker described "a business relationship". She explained this: "I'm their source of help. When something is in the offing, like a holiday, they bombard me with calls. They persist, they ring to ask me when am I calling, what day, and what time? They are very precise about timing, and I dare not be five minutes late, or I get a sarcastic greeting like 'Oh, you made it then!' or 'Good afternoon' if it's morning. I find it best to ignore it. When I visit, they are always sitting by the fire waiting for me.

It's always got to be like that. They don't like me to come un-announced. It's an appointment system only. And it's business on their terms".

The social worker as informal official

Charles Deacon's social worker felt he was seen as "an official with a specific job to do, i.e., to fix things and quickly, immediately if possible". It was a friendly relationship too, as it included "affable chats about news and current affairs", but it was circumscribed:"I am kept in my place, I mustn't get too close".

Edward Hayes' social worker made a similar point: "I'm a friendly authority person. We sort out practical things but we also have friendly exchanges". He made a similar point in relation to how Richard Evans saw him: "I'm someone who is in charge of them, over them, who has a say in whether they should remain there or not. And yet I'm free and easy with them . . . we do things together, and have fun".

Doreen Gilmore's social worker echoed this view: "We are on first name terms and we are friendly. But I represent the office in a formal way. The social worker role implies a boundary between home and work".

The social worker as "the big gun"

This was a term used by a social worker to explain his relationship with Colin Markham: "I have a straight authoritarian role with him because he plays the others up, and he plays the centre up. I have to lay the law down, albeit reluctantly, but it is the only recourse I have in the end. It seems to work, he accepts my higher authority".

Elaine Court's social worker described herself as "an authority figure; I have power over her and attempt to control her behaviour". Elaine was frequently the centre of conflict in her group home: "She has a way of winding the others up". She was often censured by her peer group who enlisted the social worker's help in trying to browbeat her into more publicly acceptable behaviour.

Similarly, Daniel Baxter's social worker described herself as "an authority figure". Daniel confirmed this: "a junior Sister Johnson, always telling me off". Daniel had caused concern within his group because he was out of step with their routines; he would get up late, go out in the evenings without telling anyone, and would sometimes arrive home late. Daniel also presented problems because of his poor personal hygiene and his tendency to become aggressive. Somehow, he always managed to be at the receiving end of public lectures.

The social worker as a threat

Two social workers described themselves as threatening figures in service users' eyes, though this was not their intention. Ralph Walker's social worker explained what she called the "delicate area" of their relationship: "He doesn't want to accept advice because it's threatening to him, it undermines the male role. He would like to have more say in his own affairs. There ought to be things that he, as a man, could decide for himself . . . . Perhaps he resents the fact that I, as a woman, am the manager, and he would like to be in my position".

Joan Woods' social worker described their "fragile relationship": "I have to tread carefully so as not to cause a rumpus . . . Joan sees me as someone who wants to get in but who doesn't do anything anyway. I don't go very often. She doesn't want me there". The issue was personalised because the social worker represented authority, and Joan's domestic circumstances with two elderly, frail friends were very precarious. She appeared to feel threatened by the implied authority element in the relationship, and reacted negatively to the social worker. Nevertheless in the research interview, though dismissive of the social worker's achievements, Joan did see the latter as an appropriate source of help.

The social worker as a friend

The term "friend" was the one used most often by social workers to describe their role with service users. This applied in twenty of the fifty relationships studied.

For example, Fiona Appleby's social worker described himself as her friend: "I'm a friend to talk things over with, to tell things to — what they are doing, what they intend to do, experiences they have had in the day, who they've seen, and to recount experiences from the past".

Another example was Norma Jones. Her social worker described their relationship: "I'm a friend to her; we have heart-to-heart talks, we talk things over woman to woman. Edgar and Robert are friends, and she needs my friendship. We do special things together, like shopping for clothes, and we might bring fish and chips home with us to eat together".

Similarly, Melanie Saunders' social worker described herself as a friend. "I'm definitely her friend. She calls me Daphne. She lowers any barriers there might have been. I'm usually Mrs. Morley, but she just pushes formalities away. For example, if I knock on the door while she is having a bath she will shout, 'Daphne, come on up!' She loves to have her back scrubbed − she has no inhibitions, no modesty".

Helen and Bruce Winters saw their social worker as a friend; for Helen it was a special friendship. Her social worker explained: "I'm like the central pole of her rotary washing line, the bit that stands straight when the rest gets tangled up with the day's washing". Much of their contact was social, chatting over tea: "I'm not really asked to *do* anything just *be* there, in case they have a worry".

Two more examples illustrate the same theme. Thus Maurice Dean's social worker described himself as a "friend" too: "I'm probably someone he can manipulate! I'm one of Maurice's fan club, a member of his supporters' club". And Olive Davis's social worker said: "I'm her personal friend . . . I'm someone who comes to see how they are, who cares about them, is interested in them and will do things for them. Olive likes to have a hug, and a cuddle too, it underlines the friendship".

The social worker as a close tie

In a few instances the social work relationship seemed to have become a particularly close bond; and the social worker described the bond not as friendship but more as a family tie. Three examples will illustrate this point.

Enid Walker's social worker described herself as "an older sister". She explained this: "Enid needs time, a lot of attention, undivided attention − she needs a long time to explain how she feels. She is glad of my support, she trusts me and is able to talk over anything that is worrying her ... Enid does not resent her dependency on me, she welcomes it, it makes her more viable as a person".

In Laura Vickers' case, the social worker saw herself "like a more competent daughter helping an ageing parent". Theirs was a close tie, based on long-established and frequent contact, and real feelings. The social worker explained this aspect of their relationship: "I have negotiated her out of hospital, into marriage, and through bereavement, into well adjusted widowhood, and almost complete independence. Somehow I have become an *essential* part of the scenario, certainly in Laura's eyes".

In Geoffrey King's situation the close tie evoked feelings of ambivalence, described by the social worker thus: "It is an ambivalent relationship. He is very dependent on me for help, advice, and support, but resents this dependency too. It's a bit like a marital relationship – I'm the most important person in his life, and the person closest to him, and I get the most abuse too! But I have stood the test of time, I've been with him through all his troubles, and I've never been disloyal".

Negotiating closeness

As already mentioned, social workers described themselves as "friends" of twenty out of the total of fifty service users in the study. For everyone else, relationships were more complicated, and were not just based on informality and fun. When social workers really thought about their involvement in people's lives and how they in turn were perceived, they were able to identify a range of feelings and reactions. Closeness, or fear of closeness, brought reactions on both sides. Some service users felt undermined or threatened, others seemed dependent, and some expressed ambivalent feelings towards their social workers. Social workers noted how some people negotiated their own boundaries through insistence on "business on their terms" and strict adherence to appointments. Some social workers followed this policy themselves, underlining the boundary between social and work-based relationships.

The relationships described here were not "planned"; they had simply evolved over time. Often social workers had not previously thought about the nature of their involvement; they and the people with whom they worked had slipped into ways of relating with each other which suited them. Standing back in the research interview, and taking time to reflect on their task as social workers proved useful. It allowed them time and space to "make sense" of their involvement and think about what they were doing. This was a luxury. Yet their work at the front line was tough and challenging. In the absence of a regular time slot for this purpose, social workers welcomed this one-off opportunity to explore their work.

Part Two

Implications of research findings for front line staff

CHAPTER EIGHT

Implications of the research

Discussion of findings

Social workers emerged as central support figures in the lives of the people in this study, being the human part of a community care policy-in-practice. In his early study, Edgerton (1967) suggested that ex-patients required the good offices of a "benefactor". The social workers in this study appear to have taken on such attributes: "These benefactors provide welcome assistance with the practical difficulties of coping with everyday problems . . .".

The present study has indicated a primary role for generic social workers in working with people with mental handicaps. The people in the research group became part of mixed case loads, an arrangement which seemed to suit both parties well. The study has also highlighted the frequency of contact, the regular and predictable nature of social worker-service user meetings, and the long-term nature of the relationship. Social workers became part of people's "structure for coping", in Bayley's (1973) terms, offering help that fitted into a daily and weekly timetable of routines.

The present study has distinguished the formal aspects of the social worker's role from its informal aspects. The formal features of the role comprised a range of supportive tasks, including practical and financial help, mediation, provision of services, crisis intervention, and personal advice. Social workers were involved in all aspects of people's lives and, in the context of a long-term relationship, informality became the norm and contact took on features of friendship.

A particularly interesting finding was the individuality of the social worker-service user contact. It is a point noted by Tyne (1978) and highlighted in the present context. Although social workers may have been designated to work with a group they did not relate primarily to the group as a unit, or adopt a standardised way of relating to the group's individual members. Instead, they built up a special, unique relationship with each member of each group, and even with each friend or partner in close friendships or marital relationships. This tendency to individualise contact suggests a move towards the benefactor status; ensuring an individual contact, or confidante, for each person. This may be a major factor in the successful adjustment made by service users to their new lives in the community.

As Tyne (1978) points out: "The relationship with the social worker ... is then a complex one which cannot be described as 'dependency'". The findings of the present study confirm the complexity of this key relationship. Social workers each described their relationships with each of the people with whom they worked: their descriptions were entirely personal to each service user, regardless of what other relationships co-existed within the same household. It is this tendency towards the personalised contact which makes this relationship not simply one of dependency. The closeness, the informality, and the long-term nature of the contact led sometimes to friendship; to reciprocal relationships developing between social workers and some service users.

It is this individualised contact that distinguishes this field of social work. It brings rare opportunities for social workers to share, and to experience, the lives of the people with whom they work. They become, then, more than "someone to turn to": they become, instead, part of life.

Implications for social workers

The research study, at one level, gives a positive account of social work involvement. It does, however, also highlight some issues of interest for social workers and others in the front line of services:

the prolonged dependency of people with mental handicaps on their social workers, and the effects of this on both parties;

the "friendship" myth;

the exclusivity of contact, and its impact on people's lives;

the risks involved for people with mental handicaps in living in the community;

social work's monopoly in this area of work?

Each of these areas will be discussed separately, and the implications for social workers drawn out.

Prolonged dependency

Long-term contact can bring its own rewards, both for people with mental handicaps and their social workers, in terms of closeness and warmth. It can also bring prolonged practical and emotional dependency; service users perceiving social workers as competent, supportive, and knowledgeable. This dependency could conceivably lessen people's opportunities to grow, learn, and develop as separate and autonomous individuals. It could also take its toll on social workers who might, over time, come to feel an increasing rather than a lessening sense of responsibility (Mason, 1983).

The role of "benefactor" suggests a paternalistic stance. In his later studies of the same research cohort, Edgerton found that benefactors became less important over time, and a "network of friends" (Edgerton and Bercovici, 1976) and people's "own resources" (Edgerton, Bollinger, and Herr, 1984) became more telling factors in community adaptation. This suggests that although a benefactor may be important in the early stages of community living, that influential role appropriately lessens in due course as people make new contacts and begin to find their own feet.

In this study, relatively long-term relationships between social workers and service users were fostered. There were many good reasons for this in terms of building a relationship of trust and encouraging a sense of security, and most people seemed to welcome the closeness of their contact with their social workers. The challenge remains to find ways of enabling people to develop their own inner resources through a relationship of trust, without inadvertently reducing their motivation to do so or undermining their own efforts through continual availability and helpfulness. This dilemma is not peculiar to social work; it is shared by parents and other front line staff.

There is another aspect of the dilemma. Emotional dependency can bring its own rewards and results. It can make social workers feel necessary and service users feel valued. No-one necessarily has any motivation to make changes. Perceived dependency can be positively rated even on a long-term basis, as in the situation cited in the research report: "Enid does not resent her dependency on me, she welcomes it, it makes her more viable as a person".

In short-term case work, or counselling, "dependency" characterises a phase in which people work on some personal issues whilst in a warm, supportive relationship. This is seen as a necessary stage on the way towards greater personal autonomy and responsibility. In long-term, open-ended work with people, dependency may not be so easily accommodated as a phase; it may become a feature of the long-term relationship itself. If there is no ultimate goal of autonomy or independence, then there may be no phasing out of dependency. Prolonged dependency of this kind may not be helpful to either participant, but it can happen without people noticing. Good supervision and support of workers in the front line could help with this, at least in bringing the issue into their awareness. Only then can it begin to be dealt with.

Reducing the frequency or level of contact can be difficult. It can lead to anxiety for both parties about the consequences of increased independence; and can lead to feelings of insecurity, abandonment and loss, and a sense of betrayal or rejection on the part of service users. Withdrawal needs to be carefully planned and timed, and attempted only when a reliable support network has been fostered and established.

The friendship myth

Many social workers in this study described themselves as "friends" of the people with whom they worked. Some service users shared this view, and came to see their social workers as their "friends" too. Friendship suggests warmth, mutual liking, and reciprocity; and some of the relationships were described in these terms.

Such a tendency is not peculiar to this study or to this branch of social work. In other areas of long-term social work, friendship and friendliness also characterise the contact between worker and client (Sainsbury, Nixon, and Phillips, 1982). It was found in the Sainsbury study that friendly feelings were based on personal liking rather than on the material or practical help provided, and that clients felt that friendliness increased steadily over time.

In the present study an informal approach, a long-term perspective, and the all-embracing nature of the contact led people to form close relationships. Friendships between paid professionals, or staff, and service-users can be seen as helpful if it means that friendship skills can be learned and transferred elsewhere (Atkinson, 1987). A relationship of this kind may be less than helpful, however, if it precludes opportunities for service users to meet other people and to create friendships where intimacy and reciprocity are explicit goals.

The notion of the social worker-service user relationship as a "friendship" may be seen as a myth if it does not entail intimacy and reciprocity. Sometimes people with few, or no, friends may come to redefine existing contacts as friends as a way of enhancing their personal circumstances. In research interviews there may well be a tendency for respondents to offer an improved version of their lives, and to have one friend, albeit a social worker, may be more enhancing to their self-image than to admit to having no friends.

The "myth" of friendship, if such it is, may be exposed in the fullness of time; for example, when social workers are promoted and leave fieldwork, or obtain a job elsewhere and leave the area. The test of friendship is whether it persists in spite of a major change of circumstances. If it does not persist, is that yet another personal loss in the lives of individuals who may already have experienced the loss of other key people?

Some friendships had persisted through major changes. Ada Smith, for example, mentioned Mr. Carter: "We're not under him now. He calls us friends". Even after the death of Mrs. Hart, his social worker, Maurice Dean remained "a friend of her family". Others, however, had not withstood the friendship test. Social workers lived on in people's memories, but they were no longer in touch.

What are the guidelines in this area? The evidence from this study and elsewhere (Sainsbury, Nixon, and Phillips, 1982) suggests that frequent and close contact between social workers and service users will often lead to friendship. Two points can be made here. First, the nature of the relationship can be made explicit to service users from the beginning: so that, if it is to be a "strictly business" relationship or a short-term, time-limited experience, this is stated and friendship myths are not encouraged. Secondly, the social worker-service user friendship itself, if such it becomes, can be used to encourage other friendships; through personal introductions, role modelling, and practising and transfer of friendship skills.

Exclusivity of contact

The people in the research study had previously lived in long-stay hospitals. Their experiences of "block treatment" and "routinisation" contrasted with the individualised and personal contact offered them in their own homes by social workers. It was not surprising that their feelings sometimes turned to friendliness, and a working relationship to them became a friendship.

A close personal relationship between two people can become exclusive. There may be no incentive, from the service user's point of view, to avoid or reduce this exclusivity. A relationship with a social worker, however close, warm, and caring, might not seem much to sustain someone emotionally; yet some relationships in the research appeared to do just that. Letters to their social workers from Joyce Hardcastle ("I am thinking about you every day and night") and Laura Vickers ("I miss you a lot") suggested this degree of exclusivity.

An exclusive relationship can, as already suggested, restrict service users' opportunities to meet new people and form reciprocal relationships elsewhere. Any tendency to exclusivity may be counteracted by joint work on preserving existing relationships, re-making links with family and friends from the past, widening the current circle of contacts, and facilitating new relationships (Atkinson and Ward, 1986). A network of relationships, which includes non-handicapped and local people, can not only reduce dependency and counteract exclusivity, it can also encourage social integration.

Risks

The research study, as previously stated, considered two groups of people: those living in minimum support groups; and those living in their "own homes". The minimum support groups were meant to be low risk living arrangements; the "own home" option, by comparison, a high risk undertaking.

Most of the people studied, who had left hospital in the years 1971–1981, had been selected, trained, and placed in minimum support groups: a model designed as a low risk venture in community living, with specified safeguards built-in. It was meant to incorporate peer group interdependence, regular help from a social worker, financial and practical support, and the provision of new, and safe, domestic equipment. Some risks were anticipated and efforts made to minimise them. There was, for example, little opportunity for people to get into financial difficulty, people were assured of company, and the houses in which the groups lived were kept warm, comfortable, in good decorative order, and relatively safe.

The study also included, however, ten people who had side-stepped the official route out of hospital, and had gone instead straight into homes of their choice. They set up home alone, or with a friend or spouse. The lack of initial preparation, and the absence of continuing control, meant that some of these people lived in cold, poorly decorated homes, with reduced leisure options. They disregarded some of the usual departmental safeguards, for example, by using paraffin heaters, keeping open fires, and buying second-hand electrical and gas equipment. Their domestic situations seemed almost to maximise the risks involved in community living.

In practice, people living in both types of setting had experienced incidents such as small fires, burst pipes, and domestic accidents. People in minimum support groups had less financial worries (and less freedom) and enjoyed a more comfortable life style. Their home life was, however, sometimes characterised by group tension and conflict, and occasional violence. On the other hand, those self-selected and self-motivated people who had opted for greater independence had financial responsibility (and financial worries) and lived in less comfort. But they were spared the emotional intensity of group living, and largely avoided interpersonal conflict.

The minimum support group model was built on the principle of people's interdependency; when it worked well it promoted peer group support and a cooperative atmosphere. But there were many instances in which confined group living promoted instead dissent, conflict, and even violence. These factors seemed potent in determining individual outcome: the well-supported and structured minimum support groups lost, or shed, people; whereas the small, semi-autonomous "own homes" remained intact. Several people who experienced conflict left their group homes to live alone, or with a marital partner or friend.

Did social work practice vary between the two groups? Were the relationships between service users and social workers influenced by the different settings and their perceived inherent risks?

Social work practice

There were two noticeable differences in social work practice in relation to members of minimum support groups and people living in their own homes. One significant difference was highlighted earlier (see page 30), when it was seen that the lack of departmental guidelines on work with people in their own homes led to social workers and service-users negotiating for themselves, and sometimes re-negotiating, the nature of the contact. People's aspirations towards greater independence led sometimes to financial difficulties and personal hardship, and the social workers concerned had to negotiate a balance between advice and practical help, and perceived "interference" in people's private lives.

Secondly, the resolution of conflict between members of minimum support groups became an area of crisis intervention for some social workers, but was an aspect of practice not needed in working with individuals in two-person "own home" households.

Relationships

The differences in practice described, and the level of risk anticipated or perceived by social workers, were reflected in the relationships which developed between people. The expected level of "high risk" for people living in their own homes had two consequences. One consequence was that all the more negative reactions recorded by service users and pinpointed by social workers were made in relation to people living in their own homes. Social workers appeared as "a threat" to Ralph Walker and Joan Woods; the social worker's role being seen by them as an undermining one which interfered with their personal efforts to get on with their lives.

The converse held true too. The closest relationships between service users and social workers, described in the research account as "close ties", all involved people living in their own homes. Long-term, close, and unstructured contact between people could, it seemed, move even beyond friendship into specially close bonds.

The issues of prolonged dependency and exclusivity were apparent in this context, and were thrown into sharp relief by the reactions of people living in their own homes. Service users who resisted dependency and avoided exclusivity could, in the end, develop personal inner resources which could lead to an alternative support network. Maurice Dean, for example, counted his social worker as just one member of his "supporters club". On the other hand, someone who developed a friendship link or close tie with a social worker risked the loss of opportunities for personal development and new relationships; and, ultimately, the loss of even that special person. Laura Vickers' social worker had become an *"essential* part of the scenario" leaving little room for other friends; and Geoffrey King's social worker saw herself as "the most important person in his life."

A social work monopoly?

This study was about social workers in relation to people with mental handicaps living independently in the community. This is not to suggest that social workers should be the only people involved in supportive roles and relationships with people, or that community living should be reserved for people able to achieve a high degree of independence. The opening chapter of this book set a scene far wider than social work; one which included all "front line staff", and involved service users, or consumers, with varied handicaps and backgrounds, including people with very severe difficulties.

The support offered by social workers in this study was practical and emotional. Their practical involvement in day-to-day social and domestic events took them into realms of activity not peculiar to social work. Other front line staff are similarly well placed to help and advise people on a range of personal and household activities.

In terms of emotional support, the social work task took on aspects of a counselling role. This was particularly apparent in the examples given in the text of "personal help and support", where people discussed their lives, present and past, and looked at making changes. This "direct counselling role" (NISW, 1982) is seen as part of the social work task, but is not exclusive to social work. Counselling can be seen as "a way of being" with another person (Rogers, 1961; Murgatroyd, 1985) and, on that basis, is a helping activity open to other staff at the front line of services.

In terms of personal involvement and moves towards friendship, this is not a social work monopoly either. Close, day-to-day contact between staff and service users, whatever the designation of staff, may lead people into working relationships which take on aspects of friendship. Arguably this is a more likely outcome for staff who live in the same locality as the homes they visit, and who share access to local networks, than it is for social workers who are geographically distant and who visit more rarely.

The rest of Part Two is a discussion of a wider context. It takes up the theme of relationships, from the main body of the research report, and explores two key aspects of relationships which emerged from the study. Chapter Nine looks at the rewards and the pitfalls inherent in relationships between "front line staff" and the consumers of services. Chapter Ten looks at the fraught area of relationships between householders, and how front line staff are, voluntarily or involuntarily, intimately involved in these. Implications for the appropriate training and support of staff are drawn out in both key areas of interest. The subsequent discussion draws further examples from the research project, which included home helps and volunteers as well as social workers, and widens the context further by drawing on examples from other studies.

Finally, Chapter Eleven draws together some suggestions for good practice in this area of work. Although derived from this study of mainly social workers, the suggestions apply across the board to other front line staff.

CHAPTER NINE

Relationships between staff and service users

Negotiating difficulties

In Chapter One the point was made that the job of offering support to people with mental handicaps living in the community may be fraught with difficulty. This is because front line staff are working in direct and close contact with service users in aspects of everyday living, where feelings may run high and misunderstandings may occur.

Some examples of what can go wrong may help to illustrate this point. The "going wrong" might be written into the script from the outset if service users do not actually welcome the attentions of staff members in the first place. A note in one person's case file in the research project made this point: "When the home help retired Doreen wanted to manage things herself, she didn't want any more 'help'". A social worker interviewed during the study commented about Gerald Turner's view of his home help: "He doesn't get on with her, he sees her as interfering. He hadn't wanted her to call at all, and wants her out". Joan Woods spoke for herself: "If I could get out shopping I wouldn't have a home help".

If front line workers get beyond the point of initial mistrust on the part of service users, there are still delicate areas which need to be negotiated with care. Whose home is it anyway? And whose life? Where is the fine line drawn between being helpful and supportive, and being interfering and undermining?

A home-maker, in the research project, described her delicate role in relation to some of the people she visited daily: "With Martin, I have to *nag* him to get him to do his share of the housework. I *lecture* Elaine about her behaviour; she is unreasonable in her demands on the others, and won't shut-up. On the other hand, Elaine talks to me on a day-to-day basis, and rings me at home for advice. When Martin got lost, I went out in the car, found him and brought him home".

A social worker explained the difficulties faced by a home help in dealing with three very independently-minded friends who lived together: "Mrs. Lewis gives personal advice (not welcomed!) on budgeting, hygiene and cleanliness. She has encouraged them to save towards regular bills so as to avoid their usual panics, but to no avail. She has tried, unsuccessfully, to re-establish a household kitty. Hers is a difficult role; she has to be tactful and diplomatic yet improve and maintain standards. They shut her in the kitchen once during a row, and she was very frightened".

Robert Harper's home help "meant well" when she picked his ripe strawberries. The social worker described what happened: "The garden is his pride and joy. He plans it, says when it's time to sow things and when to pick them. He had a dispute with the home help when she picked his strawberries. He was very angry. I had to have a word with her".

What happens when front line staff impose their own standards on people? Nigel Malin (1983) gives an example from one of the group homes he studied in Sheffield. The support worker, in this instance, "went too far in imposing her standards, in criticising how residents spent their personal monies and how they pursued their leisure activities, for example, Beryl's embroidery. 'I told you to do each of those flowers a different colour, not the same.' At times such incidents caused difficulties, for if this home help found that residents were behaving contrary to the plans set for them, she would immediately report the incident to the social work assistant who would be expected to take action. For example, she reported that residents were being 'devious' − 'they rush through their work in the morning and soon as I've gone, on goes the TV, but they know when I'm returning in the afternoon like I do sometimes and its always off in time'".

The conflicts which arise may be due, in part, to people's different perceptions. People living in an ordinary house in the community might well value most highly their freedom, independence, and range of choices. From a staff point of view, cleanliness, orderliness, and conformity may be desired goals. The present author has argued elsewhere that front line staff may try to create "the model client" in the community (Atkinson, 1983); the community equivalent of the hospital's "model patient".

Nigel Malin (1983) quotes the aims stated by some of the support staff in his study. These were: to create a home; to improve residents' quality of life; to increase residents' happiness; to make residents live as independently as possible; to help residents live a normal life; to help residents function as a family.

In attempting to achieve these aims, staff members could easily encroach too far into people's personal space. A home help in the Sheffield study: "was disliked by at least some of the residents, probably because her attitude to them was both overbearing and overprotective, and they had little opportunity to learn new skills ..." (Malin, 1983).

The formal role of front line staff may be set out in job descriptions, and people may have their allotted check lists of tasks and activities. The formal role, however, is complicated by people's perceptions of it. Staff who perceive the role as one of enabling people to achieve personal goals and facilitating desired changes and choices may meet with little conflict, at least from the service users. Staff who perceive their role in terms of care and control, and avoidance of risk, however, may find themselves resented by people who want to test the limits of freedom, independence, and autonomy.

There may be a further dimension to the conflict. Staff who produce "model clients" and "model homes" may be in conflict with service users but they may actually be in line with departmental policy and may be approved of. Staff who experience role conflict may be those who adopt the role of enabler and facilitator. This role, though it may meet with the approval of service users, may incur the disapproval of an organisation which prefers tidy people in neat houses.

How do staff feel about their roles?

The situation is further complicated by people's feelings and personal reactions to one another. On the one hand, people with mental handicaps might feel frustrated in their wishes to branch out and explore new possibilities in their lives, and may begin to resent efforts of staff to restrict their opportunities and protect them from risks. On the other hand those staff members, who are being restrictive and protective, may be so because of their own feelings. People who feel isolated, vulnerable, and responsible in their work situations are likely to avoid risks, play safe, and "cover" themselves.

Feeling isolated

Working in or visiting small, dispersed houses in the community is a very different experience from being part of a team in a hostel or hospital. In the community setting there may be no natural peer group with which to relate, nor easy access to a senior for support. Staff at the front line often have to think quickly and make their own decisions.

What are they supposed to be doing? What does "support" mean? These are important questions. The social workers in the research study were, as individuals, finding their own answers; but, in the absence of any clear guidelines, they were confronted with day-to-day dilemmas in their work. They felt isolated. The research interview itself was a rare opportunity to reflect on their work and what it meant.

Other front line staff may, as Jan Porterfield (1985) points out, be left to get on with the job. Without proper support and encouragement, and contact with colleagues, they can begin to feel isolated and uncertain about what they should be doing. The front line of services can be a lonely place; and staff can easily conclude that no-one cares much about what they do, providing nothing goes wrong.

Feeling vulnerable

Staff may feel vulnerable for several reasons. They may feel pressure to succeed in their task of "making a go" of a local service. They may feel that the success (or failure) of the project is very much tied to their own success (or failure) as support workers. They may feel anxious about the prospect of "failing", or fear that risks will rebound on them.

The author has described elsewhere (Atkinson, 1982b) her own feelings of "inadequacy" and of "being outmanoeuvred" in her role as social worker; a feeling of vulnerability brought about by always "being the loser" in social encounters.

Feeling responsible

In her study of some group homes in Avon, Kate Mason (1983) describes the key workers' feeling of "total and never ending responsibility which can be so wearing". Key workers apparently felt almost total responsibility for people, over long periods of time, and in most of the key areas of their lives. They provided emotional support, mediated with neighbours, and intervened in crises. They saw no end to, nor even any lightening of, this level of involvement; the demands, and the responsibility, they felt would continue indefinitely.

Staff who feel isolated, vulnerable, and responsible may not be well placed to provide the kind of sensitive help that service users are looking for. The formal role of these staff may be to help and support people in their homes and neighbourhood, enabling them to develop skills and independence, make friends and, overall, to enjoy a good quality of life. To perform this role well front line staff need to feel supported themselves. Without adequate support: "staff feel isolated and neglected, sickness and absence rates increase and minor annoyances become major problems" (Mansell and Porterfield, 1986).

How can staff be helped to feel less isolated, vulnerable, and responsible?

It is not, perhaps, surprising that staff working in small dispersed houses in the community can come to feel isolated. There is no natural support network of colleagues for them to plug in to, so support has to be specially built-in. Staff teams, comprising colleagues from several houses in a larger area, may have to be created. Support is needed from above too, so a responsible senior person should be there to offer sensitive guidance, advice, feedback, and positive monitoring of their work.

Staff begin to feel less vulnerable when they have colleagues with whom to relate, and senior staff who can offer support and guidance. It helps when they know what is expected of them, and clear guidelines are laid down. Staff are likely to feel less vulnerable if they feel adequately prepared for the job; through prior training and an induction period. The work is demanding, and sometimes wearing; staff can, and do, run out of energy, enthusiasm, and ideas. They then become vulnerable again. Perhaps in-service training can help, and the chance to attend short courses off the job or to visit other projects from time to time.

Front line staff can begin to feel less responsible when they can relinquish some control over the lives of others. This process of "letting go" is not easy, and staff may need talking through it, with support built-in as they move forward. Staff who adopt the role of "friend, facilitator and advocate" (Ridley, 1985) are more likely to see people with mental handicaps as fellow citizens, able to take some responsibility for themselves, than staff who remain locked in the role of responsible carer. People need opportunities to reflect on their formal role and what this means in practice; and how their actual role performance is determined, to a large extent, by their attitudes, perceptions, and feelings about people with mental handicaps. The feeling of total responsibility is inappropriate. It reflects an underlying attitude; that people need caring for and looking after.

Positive monitoring: the manager's role

Staff feel less isolated, vulnerable, and responsible when they are in a supportive relationship with their immediate senior. Managers have a key role in setting up and maintaining this supportive relationship. A key aspect of it is positive feedback. Managers praise, and give credit for, good work. They are constructive and helpful when there are difficulties. The relationship is stronger when it works both ways; when managers seek staff members' views too and discuss a range of ideas and possible solutions with them.

A supportive relationship is extremely important, but it is not the whole solution to staff feelings of isolation, vulnerability, and responsibility. Staff also need guidance about what is expected of them and what they are meant to do. This is no easy task for managers because, as this study has shown, the way is as yet un- charted and the pitfalls are unclear. Guidance may have to emerge through continuing discussions between managers and staff, and it may have to be renegotiated in the light of experience.

This makes the situation a two-way process. Managers do not know all the answers, especially in work where staff members are involved in personal relationships with people. Staff views about their relationships count for a lot here. Part of the task of managers is to provide a supportive atmosphere in which dilemmas, doubts, and conflicts can be brought into the open. No neat set of guidelines will emerge from this process, but approaches to individual service users will evolve.

This management style and approach has been called "positive monitoring". According to Porterfield (1987) positive monitoring means that managers:

give credit for good work;

are constructive when something goes wrong;

discuss possible solutions;

seek staff views;

admit they do not have all the answers.

How can staff and service users develop positive relationships?

Difficulties *can* be smoothed out between people, especially when the people involved develop self-awareness and a heightened sensitivity towards others. Some of this has to be learned and practised, and staff members may find it a painful process. It brings its own rewards though, by enabling positive relationships to develop between people as well as mutual respect for one another.

There are many instances where staff and service users "hit it off" and develop close relationships; where the formal role gives way, to some extent, to informality, affection, and fun. One social worker in the research project described Mrs. Hart's relationship with her minimum support group: "Mrs. Hart is the key figure in the group. She keeps a maternal eye on them, without interfering, and they have total trust in her and great affection for her. She is absolutely central. She and her husband do odd jobs for them in the evening and at weekends. She's much more than a home help with three sessions a week. She's there, at the end of a phone. She thinks about them, they're like part of her family".

People in the front line may choose to drop the formalities and move towards friendship. The following examples are instances where social workers opted for informality and fun.

> Dennis Adams and Roland Masters used to go on shopping trips to a nearby city with their social worker, the day made special by morning coffee in a smart café and lunch in a pub.

> Melanie Saunders would take her social worker with her to buy new underclothes and then required that she joined her in the changing room to help her struggle into her corsets.

> Bruce and Helen Winters would invite their social worker to their special birthday tea parties.

> Gerald Turner, Eric Hastings, and Iris Barber saw their social worker on Christmas Day when he called at their house to have sherry with them.

> Edgar Carter baked cakes for his social worker to take home to her family.

This kind of informality of contact and development of friendship between staff and residents was also found by Nigel Malin in his study of group homes in Sheffield. He gave as examples of this informal relationship between people: an evening out at a pub together; reciprocal out-of-hours visits to each other's homes; and hugs, kisses, and signs of genuine mutual affection. He observed that sometimes staff acted as friends to residents as well as undertaking their more official functions: "Friendship meant taking an extra interest in the group as individuals; it meant experiencing things with as well as doing things for them. Being a friend implies a relationship built on mutual trust and liking and the close relationship that evolved reflected the presence of close patterns of personal interaction that became the foundation on which many developments were based" (Malin, 1983).

What training do staff need?

Staff need to know about personal, social, domestic, and community skills, and how to help people develop these. They also need to know how to communicate with people, and how to demonstrate, or model, a wide range of daily living skills.

Staff need to know far more than this though. They need to understand the human context within which the teaching and/or doing occurs. They need self-understanding, and a sensitivity to other people's, often unspoken, innermost feelings. Their job has much to do with feelings, and relationships between people. Training must reflect this. Many people can teach skills. But can they do so within a relationship which affords dignity and respect to the person being taught?

Local staff are the key resource in a human service. They are key figures in the household itself, and in the lives of the people who live there; and they are key figures in the world outside. Local staff, with their family, friendship, and neighbourhood ties, form the link between people living in the house and "the community". In this sense, too, training is about relationships. A training programme needs to take account of relationships between staff and service users. It also needs to look at staff as facilitators who enable people with mental handicaps to meet other people and make friends.

Self-awareness and sensitivity are also needed by staff in negotiating their own "friendships" with service users. The tendency for front line staff to develop friendships with the people with whom they work is not confined to the social workers in this one research study; it is a common human reaction to long-term, close contact with people. Nevertheless, it remains an area to be negotiated with care, and one which needs to be questioned by all the participants. Whose interests does this friendship serve? Is it of long-term value to the service user? Does it preclude people with mental handicaps finding other opportunities for making friends?

The human context

Life in the community, for people with mental handicaps, has traditionally been seen as a matter of skills and support. People who were able to acquire self-care, financial, and domestic skills were taught them by staff. Those unable to learn new skills were offered practical help and support in their homes instead.

The human context in which skills are taught and support is offered, is complex. Staff and service users are involved in close, day-to-day relationships. These may be characterised by feelings of friendship, but they can sometimes be based instead on feelings of mistrust, suspicion, or resentment. Staff and service users each have feelings and respond at a personal level. Staff need to be able to stand outside their role and identify their feelings and responses. Which ones "belong" in this situation, and which are brought from elsewhere? And, of those that do "belong", which ones are appropriate?

Staff cannot do this analysis alone. Three factors are necessary in understanding and working within this complex situation. First, initial staff training needs to take account of the emotional aspect of the work. Well-chosen case studies can at least demonstrate to staff that there are emotional issues to be dealt with in their every-day interactions with service users. This kind of exercise can begin to raise their awareness of the human context. Later in-service training programmes can then develop this theme, encouraging staff to "stand back" from their feelings and to reflect on the dynamics of their relationships with the people with whom they work.

Secondly, team meetings or staff support groups can provide a regular forum in which relationships can be discussed. In local, dispersed housing schemes, there may not be an obvious team structure. It may need to be created. This could be part of the manager's role; to create a "team" and ensure it has opportunities to meet regularly.

Thirdly, managers have a key role to play in the process of understanding human relationships: providing a supportive relationship with staff in which emotional issues can be aired and dealt with. This need is experienced by staff at all levels. The social workers in the research project needed, though did not always get, good supervision of their relationships with the service users. People involved with service users even more regularly and frequently than visiting social workers are certain, therefore, to need access to good supervision and support. Managers are themselves part of this complex human context at the front line of services; they support the supporters.

CHAPTER TEN

Relationships at home: the role of staff

A key role for staff

This chapter focuses on relationships within the home and how these, or the lack of these, can help determine the richness or impoverishment of people's lives. Living with other people does not guarantee close, positive, and supportive relationships with them. For some people it is the reverse; they meet with abuse, rebuffs and, sometimes, rejection. They may long for a home of their own, where silence and solitude can seem preferable to daily taunts from household companions. Living alone is not easy either, however, as some people have found to their cost. People living alone may face isolation and loneliness, and may have no means of making contact with others.

There is a key role for staff working with people with mental handicaps in promoting and developing close, positive, and supportive relationships between people. There is a role, too, in intervening in disputes between people, where good will has gone and trust has been suspended.

Getting on together

There is some recognition now that, where people with mental handicaps are to live together in small groups, it is as important that they like each other and get on well together as it is that they are able to carry out a range of personal, social, domestic, and community skills. However, the selection of people for group homes has traditionally been based on an assessment of each person's competence in the most common everyday living skills. Until recently little attention has been paid to what Nigel Malin (1983) calls the "group harmony" factors, although an earlier report from the field had suggested that:

"Rehabilitation is much more about emotions and relationships than about social and domestic skills." (Atkinson, 1980).

What are the factors which promote "group harmony"? There seem to be six of them:

household composition built around *existing friendships;*

compatibility between members of the household;

personal *motivation* to succeed;

joint commitment to the project;

willingness of people to *share;*

an atmosphere of *trust.*

These factors are more easy to identify retrospectively, following an individual or group breakdown or "failure", than they are to establish at the outset. Looking back on the ruins of someone's life, or on the remains of a group, it is possible to note the absence of group harmony-promoting factors. What is more difficult is to identify and promote these factors at the beginning of a group's life; to insist on their presence. This is because, with one exception, they are intangible. How can the degree of compatibility between a group of people be assessed? How can their motivation and commitment be measured? How can their willingness to share be identified? And how can an atmosphere of trust be recognised?

The one "concrete" factor is the value of building households around existing friendships. This is not always possible but, where it is, it also takes care of the intangible factors on the list. People who are friends already are usually compatible when sharing a home; and the friendship is presumably based on sharing, trust, and commitment. The following example illustrates how group harmony can be promoted, in practice, by attention to established friendships:

"In Edgar's group ... the three householders are good friends. Edgar and Robert were friends for years in hospital, and now Norma has become a friend too. They go together when Edgar visits his family in another town: 'All three of us go. We go together. I always take them with me, I don't like leaving them behind. They go and see Charles and them while I see Mum and Dad. I don't like going on my own, it's not nice leaving Norma and Robert back here.' The principle of sharing is well-established in this group home. They share the decisions ('we talk it out between ourselves'), they share the budgie ('he belongs to all of us'), and they share the chores ('we all help'). This companionship serves them well, and each member of this threesome seems to enjoy a full and active life both at home, and out and about in the community." (Atkinson and Ward, 1986)

Friendship is a sound basis for promoting group harmony. It also has great significance for the people concerned. Having at least one close friend or companion seems crucial to the well-being of people with mental handicaps living in the community. The research project confirmed this view: "Such close relationships seem to be both enduring and special. They endure beyond the change of setting, and they confer special survival abilities on the involved parties. Even if other factors are negative, the existence of one close tie can sustain a person through many ups and downs in the community" (Atkinson, 1984).

A close relationship entails companionship between people. The quality of someone's life can be greatly enriched by having a companion to share with, have fun with, and go out and about with. The "friendship" may be a marital relationship and the "companions" husband and wife, as in the following example.

"Ralph and Enid, a married couple, spend a lot of their time out and about together: 'We go shopping together. In the summer, on Sundays, we sometimes go for a walk in the park together. We've got some friends where we used to live, called Mr. and Mrs. Armstrong, and we pop round there sometimes. Mr. Armstrong answers the door and says "Hello, come on in." We go in then for a chat.'" (Atkinson and Ward, 1986).

What happens to people with mental handicaps who through choice, chance, or necessity live alone? They are outside the framework of assured company and the possibility of developing in-house friends and companions. How do they fare? Not surprisingly, experiences vary between people, as the following extract illustrates. It describes the situations of three people in the study who lived alone.

"They do not, therefore, have home-based relationships. Although Geoffrey chose to live alone, he now feels the absence of company: 'It's very difficult being a handicapped person. A handicapped person shouldn't live alone. How do you expect a handicapped person to live outside?' Two people left their group homes in order to live alone. They feel positively about leaving behind the tensions of group home life, and concentrate their energies on building up outside contacts. Maurice, for example, comments on his approach to living alone: 'I don't stay here all weekend, I go out. I go on my bike to see Doreen and them, or to have a drink in the pub'." (Atkinson and Ward, 1986).

Falling out

Group homes were established with the best of intentions; to enable people to live in a shared household where mutual help and support, and easy companionship, were readily available. Group homes were built on two principles: peer group support; and the inter-dependence of group members. Thus it was expected that people would share the day-to-day tasks and, where necessary, would help one another. People would be able to turn to one another for friendship and companionship, enjoying the support and company of household companions.

It seems a worthy aim to establish households promoting mutual help and support, sharing together, and being friends. Sometimes the "right mix" of people is found, and they live in harmony in their group homes. Often, however, it seems that there are difficulties. Life in a small group can be restrictive, irksome, and hazardous. Some people appear not to fit in; they may become first the group scapegoat and later the group reject. Other people outgrow their groups, rejecting their companions and seeking their fortunes in homes of their own (Atkinson, 1983).

Interpersonal difficulties are likely to occur in any small group. People living together in a small group, and possibly spending their days together too, are likely to experience conflicts. Alan Tyne (1978) noted the "frequent upsets within the group", the "troubles which ruffle the calm from time to time", and the "periodic upheavals" caused by "tensions". Similarly, Nigel Malin (1983) noted "many instances of petty quarrelling" as well as "more hard edged conflict" between people in group homes. Some people in Kate Mason's study (1983) "admitted to tensions, and talked of their 'ups and downs'".

What are the upsets which occur? What causes the tensions? Does petty quarrelling matter? How do people cope with periodic upheavals? What happens when there is hard edged conflict? It is possible to look at the consequences of such interpersonal conflict both in terms of its impact on individuals and its impact on the group. There are four areas of interest:

the isolated person within the group;

the person who is rejected by others;

the person who displays disruptive behaviour;

group tension and conflict.

The isolated person

Two people from the research project, Richard Evans and Dennis Adams, illustrate how it is possible to live with others, yet be alone. Richard lived in a group home, but remained isolated: "Tensions remain with the group ... with four separate individuals leading rather different lives, and personalities and temperaments somehow failing to match. Richard has no friends. His household companions are just that and no more. In interview he commented: 'We do try to make an effort to get on. I try to keep me pecker up'. He does not enjoy the group tensions, and looks forward to getting away from the difficulties when he visits his sister" (Atkinson, 1984).

According to a note in his case file, Dennis Adams was "the third person in a triangular system, Isabel and Roland excluding him from their close relationship. He has no role, no set duties and no home-based friend. The effect on him of the changed group dynamics is striking, and Dennis shuffles his way around looking for all the world like a 'down-and-out'."

The rejected person

What happens when someone, for whatever reason, is rejected by other members of a group? The experiences of Glenda Potts and Arthur Stott, taken from the research findings, illustrate what can happen.

In Glenda's case it was some time before staff began to realise there were problems. "The home help and social worker began to suspect she was being mistreated, that Helen and Bruce were treating her badly, refusing her food and making her spend her own money on groceries. Certainly Glenda was showing signs of unhappiness; she looked 'unwell and unhappy' and had taken to spending her spare time in the village cafe." (Atkinson, 1984).

Life was difficult for Arthur too, as the following extract illustrates: "Arthur is not included in anything much at home, as he is out-of-step with the rhythm of the household imposed by

Doreen, and subscribed to by the others. Arthur, described by an earlier social worker as 'rather timid, quietly spoken and of a gentle disposition', is bullied by a domineering Doreen. They row quite frequently as Arthur resists her imposed routines. Thus it is that Arthur finds himself excluded, cooking separately for himself, a scene captured in his case notes: 'Arthur was sitting huddled in the corner of the kitchen watching his eggs boil for tea, while all the others were in the sitting room entertaining friends'" (Atkinson, 1986).

The person with disruptive behaviour

Usually people become difficult and disruptive because they are unhappy where they are, and want to leave. This may well be the fate, in time, of people like Glenda Potts and Arthur Stott who are rejected by others. Other people might "outgrow" the group home (Atkinson, 1983) becoming increasingly antagonistic towards their companions in a bid for greater independence.

People do leave group homes, sometimes going to a more sheltered environment like a hostel or lodgings, and sometimes to greater independence in a flat. In Nigel Malin's (1983) study three group members were moved out of their respective group homes after a period of time in which they were aggressive and disruptive, did not get on with the others, and were caught stealing. Two people moved into a hospital, the third to a hostel. Alan Tyne (1978) notes that, over a period of time, people are likely to "up and leave" a group home, seeking more freedom and independence elsewhere.

Two examples from the present research illustrate how people can "act out" their feelings of unhappiness in their home environment. Bernard Chivers, the first example, felt excluded when two of his household companions, including his erstwhile friend from hospital days, decided to get married. Entries in Bernard's case notes referred to his "tantrums" and to his throwing articles of furniture around at midnight when he ran out of cigarettes; and "when walking along the road, he mutters almost continually to himself, and loud enough for passers-by to wonder whether he is speaking to them". The disruptive behaviour continued long enough for action to be taken, and Bernard moved into a more sheltered environment.

Alan Perkins, the second example, was unhappy in his group for another reason. He had wanted a home of his own and had only accepted a group home placement as a means of getting out of hospital. He adapted quickly, and "outgrew" his companions: "Alan proved to be the most competent member of the group, his frustrations towards his companions showing in outbursts of temper and occasional aggressive acts. He made no concessions to group living, he lived his own life with scant regard to the comfort or happiness of others, scattering his belongings everywhere, sleeping on the settee and tampering with electrical fittings to the extent that 'the whole house is a fire hazard'. Complaints from his household companions, together with his evident unhappiness with his lot, led to Alan moving into his own flat at last." (Atkinson, 1986).

Group tensions and conflict

It is not always possible to identify a person who is out-of-step with the group, and whose behaviour is a cause for concern. It may well be that it is the particular mix of people and personalities that sets sparks flying. It is as if the group is out-of-step with itself. Conflict is built in to the group dynamics from the outset. This does not mean that people do not play key roles in the resultant domestic dramas, because clearly they do; but it does mean that no one person can be held "responsible" all the time for the tensions that periodically surface.

The most common conflicts appear to be about who does what and who is the leader. Alarming though the disputes may be, they do allow less prominent members of the group to adopt the socially useful role of peacemaker.

Who does what disputes

Nigel Malin (1983) notes how, in one group home, "there was constant bickering between Doris Lampton and Violet Rylands as to who should be responsible for what" and how, in another group, "cooking was again the main source of contention". Sometimes people did not pull their weight and this led to conflict too; Doris Grantham, for example, "was often accused by the two older female residents of being lazy and not taking her turn".

Sometimes disputes go beyond bickering and accusations of laziness: "One of their 'who does what' sessions escalated into a full scale row, and Susan appeared at the Centre with a black eye. No-one would confess to anything, and the group closed ranks. Even Susan refused to comment. Usually life returns to normal after a few days, or sometimes weeks, of bitter exchanges and, increasingly, strike action or work-to-rule on Brenda's part. Their disputes have often been dramatic, with shouting, tears, and threats of leaving home . . ." (Atkinson, 1982a).

Leadership struggles

The issue of who is in charge can become contentious if two people contest the leadership role. This does not always happen. In Nigel Malin's (1983) study, the self-appointed leaders of the group homes were unopposed and evoked an appropriate "follower response" from others. An example was Gladys Smallfield, a leader who "evoked a 'follower' response; was respected by other residents and in the case of Beattie, the least able member of the group, provided a source of reassurance in most of her daily activities. Her patience, goodwill and tenacity were extremely valuable in the home".

What happens when two people seek to become leaders? This situation occurred in the present research project. June Barlow spent weekdays in the group home and weekends with her family. At weekends the field was left clear for Howard Bell to adopt the leadership role. He resented June's Monday-to-Friday claims to leadership. The dispute over who was in charge led to frequent rows, with both parties describing the other as "bossy". One row escalated into a physical encounter, in which June's finger was dislocated. The social worker reported in the case file: "Howard over-reacted to a situation which he had misinterpreted anyway. The situation got quickly overheated and escalated out of his control. He was upset at the time because of family troubles and was rather on edge, and prone to react rather more quickly than usual".

The role of peacemaker

Conflict between people in groups can lead to some group members adopting the role of peacemaker. Sometimes this means keeping a low profile and being neutral in disputes as in Roland Masters' case: "Throughout the discord, Roland kept the low profile he had maintained throughout his hospital career; never instigating rows, and never falling victim. Instead he maintained his pleasant demeanour, an air of strict neutrality" (Atkinson, 1984).

Sometimes the role was a more active one. A file note about William Fox's role in his group said: "This four-person group was dominated by Brenda and beset by rows. William's role in those days was that of a peace-keeper or, failing that, a calming influence on aggrieved people". Similarly, Nigel Short made a valued social contribution to his group: "It is a troubled group, conflict and dissent surfacing between the other three members and leading, at times, to distressing scenes. Nigel is the peacemaker; he dislikes conflict and tries to soothe frayed nerves" (Atkinson, 1984).

What can staff do?

Staff, whether visiting or residential, are inevitably involved in the relationships between service users. In a staffed home group counselling and role modelling can be particularly useful preventive skills which might defuse tensions before anyone reaches breaking point. These skills are useful for visiting staff to employ too, but they are likely to need skills in an additional area, that of crisis intervention.

Group counselling

There are three stages in group counselling. Firstly, members of staff themselves need to learn about group dynamics. The best way of learning about how groups operate is through being in one, and learning through experience. Only someone experienced in the workings of small groups can begin to disentangle the threads of discord between people.

Secondly, group members themselves need an opportunity to learn about group interactions and the give-and-take of shared living. They can also benefit from gaining some insight into their own role in groups, and how their behaviour has an impact on others. This crucial area of learning is best incorporated into an initial training programme. It is just as important to learn about relationships as it is to learn how to cook and shop; possibly more so. Staff members have a role in this. They may need to be innovative, using role-play, games, pictures, and video recordings to demonstrate points and help people learn about themselves and others.

Thirdly, staff have a role in continuing this learning process on the part of service users once they are living in community settings. This may take the form of weekly meetings, when people can be encouraged to air their grievances and work out constructive solutions to conflicts. Weekly meetings may be supplemented by *ad hoc* discussions about specific incidents, so that people have an opportunity to learn "on-the-spot" at the time of a dispute.

Role modelling

People coming from long-stay hospitals or hostels, to live in staffed or unstaffed houses, may bring with them an image of authoritarian behaviour. This may reflect how they were spoken to, as well as how they saw their peers treated. Some people may come to adopt a similar manner towards other group members; becoming a "group home dominant" (Atkinson, 1983). This means they are abrupt and speak sharply. They issue orders without explanation, and give advice which is not sought or welcomed. People adopting an authoritarian manner are likely to cause resentment in others; they set the scene for conflict.

How can people with an authoritarian style of behaviour learn more socially acceptable ways of relating to others? If the authoritarian style was learned through imitation of staff in one setting, then it is possible that a pleasant and caring manner can be learned in another setting. Staff members can be role models, demonstrating constructive and positive ways of relating to people. Staff can only take on this modelling role, however, if certain preconditions (already discussed) are met. To reiterate these: staff need to feel supported and that their work is valued. This comes about through good working relationships with colleagues, and through managers adopting the "positive monitoring" style of working.

Crisis intervention

A particularly difficult "crisis" for service users, especially in minimum support groups, is the internal conflict where tensions surface and angry feelings are unleashed. This kind of crisis is difficult to cope with, especially when people are used to residential staff acting as intermediaries and stepping in to restore order. The feelings, and the angry scenes, may be very frightening. People can, as described earlier, come to blows.

What can staff do when faced with such a crisis? The first step is to restore order. A known and trusted person arriving at the scene of battle can begin the process. A social worker interviewed during the present study commented how, in domestic disputes, her very presence was reassuring: "There is a good deal of trust and they will listen, eventually". The aim is to spread calm. The appearance of an apparently unruffled, trusted person can be reassuring to service users who have become alarmed by their own and other people's angry feelings.

The second step is to help people achieve a reconcilation or, failing that, a truce. A known and trusted staff member may be able to restore hurt feelings through apologies and handshakes. The resolution of the underlying difficulties is a longer-term process. It requires both the group counselling and role modelling skills outlined earlier.

Again, preconditions are necessary for staff to remain calm and reassuring, and able to offer people a chance to make up. They need knowledge: of human behaviour generally, and about the dynamics of small groups in particular. They also need personal awareness: enabling them to look calm and reassuring whatever they may be feeling like inside. Staff are more likely to feel calm and be reassuring if they are themselves well supported and confident about their work. They need the capacity to stand back, even in a crisis, neither being drawn in to the fray themselves nor being pushed into a hasty decision about the futures of any of the participants. Personal awareness of their own feelings can put the brakes on purely emotional responses to crises and allow staff time to think more coherently.

Someone to turn to?

Living in the community is, according to Edgerton (1984) a "highly complex and changing phenomenon". It is more than that. "It is also an intensely human phenomenon, filled with joys and sorrows, boredom and excitement, fear and hope" (Edgerton, 1984).

People with mental handicaps moving into, and living in, small domestic houses in local neighbourhoods, are at the front line themselves. They are at the front line of neighbourhood life. The risks are high; but so too are the rewards, if they come, of a full and rich life. The possible rewards, and the pitfalls, are many.

There are other people at the front line too: the staff whose role it is to facilitate change and enable relationships to develop. When the going gets tough, as it does at the front line, a staff member becomes that special person: *someone to turn to*.

CHAPTER ELEVEN

Conclusions: finding ways forward

Study findings

One of the most interesting findings to emerge from this study was that, contrary to expectations, life at the front line turned out to be mainly about relationships, and only partly about the acquisition of skills and the smooth running of households. Although practical help was important too, with numerous examples catalogued in the research report, even practical help and support took place within the context of long-term relationships between staff and service users. Helping to mend the fuse or to change the light bulb turned out to be the "easy bit" of the support role. Much more challenging turned out to be the whole area of negotiating boundaries within the close, intense relationships which developed between people over time.

The work hinged on that central relationship between "supporter" and "supported". It did not end there however. Staff found themselves involved in three other sorts of personal encounters: in helping to resolve differences that arose between service users who lived together; in providing opportunities for service users to develop new relationships outside the home; and in mediating between service users and other people in the neighbourhood.

"Support" in this context was about working within and through relationships. This proved to be no easy task, even for social workers familiar with case work and experienced in the use of counselling skills. Their way, however, was relatively uncharted. Departmental guidelines had anticipated that they would have a role in coordinating support to people living in group homes and in forging links with local people. Their personal involvement in close, long-term relationships was not anticipated, however, and nor was their role as peacemaker, friend-finder, or mediator.

This study of relationships has pointed to some ways forward for staff and managers at the front line of services. It has become apparent that both training and support of staff is important: but what form should this take? Some principles of good practice have emerged which will now be given brief consideration.

Training

The research report and linked discussion indicated that staff would benefit from heightened self-awareness, knowledge of human behaviour, and a set of interpersonal helping skills.

Self-awareness

Staff need opportunities to learn about themselves and their impact on other people. A heightened self-awareness is an important first step in developing an enabling and facilitative role with service users.

Time and space is needed for staff to explore and adjust their attitudes and reactions towards others. Only when personal boundaries are known and observed can other people's be respected. Staff who are aware of their own feelings are well placed to develop sensitivity towards the feelings of others.

Close, long-term relationships can be fraught with difficulties. Staff who are self-aware are more likely to find a role which is helpful and supportive rather than one which is interfering or undermining. They can guard against imposing their own standards on service users in order to create "model clients". They can avoid raising the expectations of people who begin to regard them as friends. They can work towards reducing the exclusivity of their contact with service users by enabling people to make friends elsewhere.

Self-awareness is best developed in experiential work, for example, in discussion groups, pairs work, role play, and use of video. If formal training opportunities are not available, some of this kind of work can be done informally in staff groups and teams.

Knowledge

The work is centred on relationships. Staff need to know about human behaviour and interactions between people. It helps to know about the dynamics of small groups and the factors which promote group harmony. Some knowledge of the roles people adopt in groups can help staff disentangle the threads of misunderstanding and conflict.

Skills

Five interpersonal helping modes have featured in this study:

These are:

counselling;

mediation;

role modelling;

crisis intervention; and,

group work.

Staff engaged in supporting people in the community can benefit from developing at least some minimal skills in these areas. Not everyone will want, or be in a position, to become an expert in the use of interpersonal helping skills. Nevertheless staff will continue to be faced with people's day-to-day problems and will need to respond appropriately. Misunderstandings are likely and the occasional crisis or conflict is always possible. Staff, therefore, need some tools at their disposal.

The counselling role, in the research study, involved social workers working with people with mental handicaps on a range of personal feelings and relationships. Staff and service users looked together at friendship, loneliness, trust, jealousy, loss, status, sex, marriage, jobs, retirement, and the future. Individualised contact between social workers and the people with whom they worked made these intimate discussions possible; long-term relationships engendered trust, and social workers took time to listen. Their manner was as important as their skills; they showed interest in, spent time with, and expressed warmth towards the people they were supporting.

The qualities and attributes of the counsellor form a sound basis from which to develop skills in other areas. But counselling, mediation, role modelling, crisis intervention, and group work all require more than just the right personal qualities and attributes. Training opportunities are also needed so that staff can develop their listening skills, their powers of observation, and their ability to intervene tactfully and helpfully.

Support

In order to offer support to service users, staff need to feel supported themselves. This "support" can take several forms. Training itself is important in helping staff develop their inner resources and personal coping skills. It enables them to learn about themselves, gain some knowledge of human behaviour, and acquire interpersonal helping skills.

A supportive work environment is also necessary if staff are to avoid the pitfalls identified in this study; of feeling isolated, vulnerable, and responsible; and being less effective, therefore, in providing sensitive help to service users. A supportive work environment incorporates these features:

> a supportive atmosphere – colleagues with whom to work and relate;

> team spirit – membership of a team of support workers (even if this has to be specially constructed);

> guidance about what is expected – through discussion, reflection, and negotiation;

> a responsible senior – who offers sensitive guidance, advice, and feedback;

> positive monitoring – of staff members' work;

> opportunities in the staff group – to reflect on personal attitudes, responses, and feelings;

> individual supervision sessions – with opportunities to stand back from relationships and explore them;

> staff members having a say – in decision-making, planning, and development of services.

A generic approach

This study looked at the relationships that existed between social workers and people with mental handicaps living independently in the community. What has emerged though is a set of generic training and support principles which have their origin in knowledge and understanding of people generally, not just in relation to people with mental handicaps.

The issues highlighted are not special to the mental handicap field: they are relevant in long-term support work with all people in their own homes and in developing positive relationships with them. Special knowledge of mental handicap and special training to work with people with mental handicaps were not identified as burning issues.

What became apparent instead was that staff needed opportunities to develop self-awareness, to study human behaviour more widely, and to acquire a set of interpersonal helping skills.

Someone to turn to

"Given someone to turn to for help with problems of ordinary life many mentally handicapped people can achieve considerable independence" (DHSS, 1971).

That "someone" could be a social worker, community nurse, home help, or any other designated support worker. But that "someone" needs someone else to turn to; a colleague, senior, or manager who, in turn, can be supportive. Everyone at the front line of services needs the support of "someone to turn to".

References

Anderson, D. *Social Work and Mental Handicap*. London: Macmillan, 1982.

Atkinson, D. Moving out of mental handicap hospitals. *Apex* (now *Mental Handicap*), 1980; **8**:3, 76 – 78.

Atkinson, D. Distress signals in the community. *Community Care*, 1982 (a); no. 421, 21 – 23.

Atkinson, D. Anything you can do. *Social Work Today,* 1982(b); **13**: 46, 13.

Atkinson, D. The Community – Participation and Social Contacts. *In* Russell, O., Ward, L. (Eds.). *Houses or Homes? Evaluating ordinary housing schemes for people with mental handicap.* London: CEH, 1983.

Atkinson, D. *Steps Towards Integration.* (Unpubl. M. Phil. thesis.) Southampton: University of Southampton, 1984.

Atkinson, D. The use of participant observation and respondent diaries in a study of ordinary living. *British Journal* of *Mental Subnormality*, 1985; **XXXI, I**:60, 33 – 46.

Atkinson, D. Engaging competent others: a study of the support networks of people with mental handicap. *British Journal of Social Work,* 1986; **16**, Suppl., 83 – 101.

Atkinson, D. How easy is it to form friendships after leaving long-stay hospitals? *Social Work Today*, 1987; June 15, 12 – 13.

Atkinson, D. Moving from hospital to the community: factors influencing the life styles of people with mental handicaps. *Mental Handicap*, 1988; **16**:1, 8 – 11.

Atkinson, D. Research interviews with people with mental handicaps. *Mental Handicap Research,* 1988; **1**:1, 75 – 90.

Atkinson, D., Ward, L. *A part of the community: social integration and neighbourhood networks.* London: CMH, 1986.

Atkinson, D., Ward, L. Friends and neighbours: relationships and opportunities in the community for people with a mental handicap. *In* Malin, N. (Ed.). *Reassessing Community Care.* London: Croom Helm, 1987.

Bayley, M. J. *Mental Handicap and Community Care.* London: Routledge and Kegan Paul, 1973.

Browne, E. T. *Mental Handicap: The Role for Social Workers.* Sheffield: University of Sheffield. Joint Unit for Social Services Research, 1982.

de Kock, U., Felce, D., Saxby, H., Thomas, M. Community and family contact: an evaluation of small community homes for adults with severe and profound mental handicaps. *Mental Handicap Research,* 1988; **2**:2, 127-140.

Department of Health and Social Security. *Better Services for the Mentally Handicapped.* (Cmnd. 4683.) London: HMSO, 1971.

Edgerton, R. B. *The Cloak of Competence.* Berkley: University of California Press, 1967.

Edgerton, R. B. (Ed.). *Lives in Process: Mildly Retarded Adults in a Large*

City. Monograph No. 6. Washington: American Association on Mental Deficiency, 1984.

Edgerton, R. B., Bercovici, S. M. The Cloak of Competence: Years Later. *American Journal of Mental Deficiency,* 1976; **80**, 485 – 497.

Edgerton, R. B., Bollinger, M., Herr, B. The Cloak of Competence: After Two Decades. *American Journal of Mental Deficiency,* 1984; **88**, 345 – 351.

Evans, G., Todd, S., Blunden, R., Porterfield, J., Ayer, A. *A New Style of Life. The Impact of Moving into an Ordinary House on the Lives of People with a Mental Handicap.* Cardiff: Mental Handicap in Wales, Applied Research Unit, 1985.

Faire, C. *It's Never Too Late: An Evaluation of Bath District Health Authority's "Ordinary Life Project" for Elderly People with a Mental Handicap.* Bath: Bath District Health Authority, 1985.

Felce, D. Behavioral and social climate in community group residences. *In* Janicki, M.P., Krauss, M.W., Seltzer, M.M. (eds.). *Community Residences for Persons with Developmental Disabilities: Here to Stay.* Baltimore: Paul H. Brookes, 1988.

Firth, H. *A Move to Community: Social Contacts and Behaviour.* Newcastle upon Tyne: Northumberland Health Authority, 1986.

Flynn, M. Independent living arrangements for adults who are mentally handicapped. *In* Malin, N. (Ed.). *Reassessing Community Care.* London: Croom Helm, 1987.

Gilbert, P. *Mental Handicap.* Sutton: Community Care/Business Press International, 1985.

Hanvey, C. P. *Social Work with Mentally Handicapped People.* London: Heinemann, 1981.

Hewitt, S. *The Family and the Handicapped Child.* London: Allen and Unwin, 1970.

Humphreys, S., Evans, G., Todd, S. *Lifelines.* London: King Edward's Hospital Fund, 1987.

Malin, N. *Group Homes for the Mentally Handicapped.* London: HMSO, 1983.

Mansell, J., Porterfield, J. *Staffing and Staff Training for a Residential Service.* London: CMH, 1986.

Mason, K. *An Examination of Policy and Practice Relating to Minimum Support Group Homes for the Mentally Handicapped in Avon.* Bristol: Avon Social Services Department, 1983.

Mathieson, S., Wilson, C., Jordan, P., Rowlands, C. Defining tasks: from policies to job descriptions. *In* Shearer, A. (Ed.). *An Ordinary Life. Issues and Strategies for Training Staff and Community Mental Handicap Services.* London: King's Fund Centre, 1983.

Murgatroyd, S. *Counselling and Helping.* London: British Psychological Society & Methuen, 1985.

National Institute of Social Work. *Social Workers: their role and tasks. The Barclay Report.* London: Bedford Square Press, 1982.

Porterfield, J. The staff – monitoring staff performance, training and the need for support. *In* Russell, O., Ward, L. (Eds.). *Houses or Homes?* London: CEH, 1983.

Porterfield, J. After initial training: then what! *In* Ward, L., Wilkinson, J. (Eds.). *Training for Change.* London: King's Fund Centre, 1985.

Porterfield, J. *Positive Monitoring.* Kidderminster: BIMH Publications, 1987.

Ridley, J. The challenge of change. *Social Work Today,* 1985; Sept. 16, 16 – 17.

Rogers, C. R. *On Becoming a Person.* Boston: Houghton – Mifflin, 1961.

Sainsbury, E., Nixon, S., Phillips, D. *Social work in focus: clients' and social workers' perceptions in long-term social work.* London: Routledge & Kegan Paul, 1982.

Shearer, A. *Building Community: with people with mental handicaps, their families and friends.* London: CMH & King Edward's Hospital Fund, 1986.

Thomas, D. Putting normalisation into practice. *In* Karas, E. (Ed.). *Current Issues in Clinical Psychology, No. 2.* New York: Plenum Press, 1985.

Towell, D. Foreword. *In* Ward, L., Wilkinson, J. (Eds.). *Training for Change.* London: King's Fund Centre, 1985.

Tyne, A. *Looking at Life in a Hospital, Hostel, Home or Unit.* London: CMH, 1978.

Tyne, A. *Staffing and Supporting a Residential Service.* London: CMH, 1981.

Ward, L. Issues in evaluating ordinary housing schemes. *In* Russell, O., Ward, L. (Eds.). *Houses or Homes?* London: CEH, 1983.

Ward, L. Developing a local service: what kind of training do staff need? *In* Ward, L., Wilkinson, J. (Eds.). *Training for Change. Staff Training for 'An Ordinary Life'.* London: King's Fund Centre, 1985.